Mitiblende

The Story of an American Family

Gene Hewett

979-8-9853727-6-2 (hardcover)

979-8-9853727-7-9 (paperback)

979-8-9853727-8-6 (eBook)

About The Book

Mitiblende reads like the story of a Black American family in its quest to sell or partition an heir's property legacy of 56 acres of undivided interest. The term Mitiblende (translation, make the brains grow smarter) was coined by Robert M. Pittman. The late Mr. Pittman was Joe Harris' uncle. Joe Harris is the novel's protagonist. The storyline is cast around property located in a small town rural Texas setting. Heirs property essentially represents generational wealth that has been transferred to multiple family members by inheritance, usually without a will. The deed to the property was dated August 2, 1898, from Sallie Simpson to Rosie Burse Edwards (Joe Harris' great-grandmother). The granting of the land was instead of monetary compensation and represented repayment for services rendered by Joe Harris' ancestors.

Historically, when a court ordered the partition of heirs' property by sale, the land was sold to the public. This typically happens by a mandatory sale at an auction. Often, property owners lost their family legacies and generally received a small percentage of what the land was worth – far below the property's fair market value. This has resulted in a tremendous amount of land loss among African Americans (disproportionately) and other people of color in the United States.

In many ways, the *Mitiblende* story can be characterized as semi-autobiographical. Several aspects of Joe Harris' childhood to adolescence to adulthood passage (such as names, places, and other identifying descriptors) may be fictional. However, many aspects of the journey, such as his efforts in structuring the Harris Family Tree, are factual and historical. Intertwined between the story is an evolving collage of clues presented in the form of letters, emails, teleconferences, and dialogue. For example, a letter written in 1986 by Joe Harris' Aunt Maude (the late Maudell Williams) provided clues that highlighted issues such as (a) the landlocked perimeter and (b) the lack of easement rights. In addition, Joe Harris' goal was to assist in charting a strategy to address a problem that had been lingering for decades. That problem was a tendency on the part of bordering neighbors to lay claim to the property via means such as adverse possession. When it came to implementing a course of action to address these issues Joe Harris soon found that not all clues had the same impact.

Similarities emerged when comparing the Shalene, Texas dilemma and the jigsaw puzzle approach often employed by crime scene detectives. By definition, a jigsaw puzzle is any set of varied, irregularly shaped pieces. When those pieces are properly assembled, they form a picture or map. In Henderson County, Texas, the four parcels of heirs' property are displayed in a County *Platt Map*. The map also includes a fifth parcel which represents the 25.3 acres that were relinquished to an encroaching neighbor in 1986.

A major premise of Mitiblende, is that the steps used by detective Sherlock Holmes could be of assistance in addressing the Shalene, Texas predicament. From Sherlock Holmes's perspective, the truth associated with the Shalene, Texas property could have been that it was Joe Harris' destiny to be called upon to assist in deciphering the clues. His steadfast efforts in prioritizing those clues eventually led to the unraveling of a myriad of problems linked to the property.

Mitiblende features fourteen premium royalty-free images. The novel has a traditional table of contents, a second one, titled "Musical Inspiration" (which includes QR Codes), and a third titled "Photographic Images." The images are presented at the beginning and end of each of the six chapters. Including the cover, and Acknowledgement fourteen images were selected from Getty Images and iStock photographic resources on the www.istockphoto.com website.

In the short run, the author envisions that *Mitiblende* will be made available in electronic, paperback, hardcover, and audiobook forms. In the long run, the author anticipates that it might be possible to package the story into a Hollywood movie production.

Acknowledgements

The term Mitiblende (translation, make the brains grow smarter) was coined by Robert M. Pittman. The late Mr. Pittman was Gene Hewett's uncle. Gene Hewett's role in the novel "Mitiblende" is portrayed by a character named Joe Harris (the protagonist). Mitiblende reads like the story of a Black American family in its quest to sell or partition an heir's property legacy of 56 acres of undivided interest. The process of addressing this dilemma required the kind of leadership and teamwork that is often displayed during mountain climbing expeditions. To win the game, the task of a mountaineer is simple, he or she must first reach the mountain's summit. In terms of heirs' property, participating family members had to (a) reach a consensus regarding the future direction of the property, and (b) obtain a favorable legal ruling in support of either selling or partitioning the land. An additional goal of a mountaineer is that he or she has to descend safely. From the perspective of the first cousins, the outcome of the sell versus partition matter had to be achieved in the most cost-effective manner possible.

Dylan Walsch wrote an article titled, *What mountain climbing expeditions tell us about teamwork*, (Insights by Stanford Business, May 29, 2019). In the latter article, Walsch referenced a study that reviewed decades of mountaineering data to measure how groupthink fared against top-down leadership. According to Walsch, for decades, academics had suggested a straightforward link between a group's solidarity and its success. In other words, the more a group operated with a single mind, the better the execution. However, the article concluded that (a) effective leaders must be able to make diversity important when it's needed and then (b) focus on collectivism when that is needed. In other words, it was important for leaders to match the hierarchy to the task at hand.

I am particularly grateful to Florence L. Hewett (mother), Rowena Wilson-Vaughan (sister), Lynette Griffin (sister), and Robert (Bob) Hewett (brother). To each of them, I wish to say thank you for instilling in me the confidence to know that it is possible to mount a task of this magnitude. I thank them for helping me to realize that sometimes when I least expect it, a chance encounter may unveil the promise and potential for new allies and innovative approaches. I am especially grateful to my first cousins Walter Pittman Jr., Jari Faison, Howard Pittman, James Pittman Jr., Darilyn Thomas, Connye Turner, Judlyne Lilly, and Lisa Shelvin. I have nothing but praise for Larry Blackmon and Wesley Blackmon (close friends of the family) whose steadfast efforts helped to move the process forward.

My mother, Florence L. Hewett, had several brothers and sisters. Three of those sisters as well as one brother laid the initial groundwork to either sell or partition the property. Their children, and my first cousins, then continued to pay the taxes. The first cousins later invited me to participate in the process. The initial *elder* group of three sisters and one brother included; Maudell Williams (Aunt Maude), Anne Lilly (Aunt Anne) , Geraldine Wooten (Aunt Geri), and James Pittman (Uncle Jim). In addition to Uncle Jim, three other brothers are referenced in Mitiblende. The latter family members included; Foster Pittman (Uncle Brother), Robert Pittman (Uncle Bobby), and Walter Pittman Sr. (Uncle Abbey).

I sincerely appreciate the truly generous efforts of the lead attorney who practiced law near the Florida Panhandle. In addition, I am grateful for the advice and guidance provided by Attorney Walker Smith (Second Lead Attorney) from the Southeast Texas firm. The information shared by the First and Second Lead Attorneys from the

North Texas law firm was also quite useful. I am especially grateful for the input outlined by the attorney who practiced law in a city that straddled the regional divide between South and Central Texas.

I owe a great deal of gratitude to the descendants of Rosie who entrusted me with the task of navigating towards the best possible outcome. Those second cousins included; Margaret Price, Willie Arthur Price, Diana Coutee, Shirley Davis, and Sheri Coutee

In addition to the above, I am equally indebted to the following parties for their assistance in advancing this process; Pamela Pittman, Laura Charity, and Eric Stanton

I am also thankful for the friendship, words of wisdom, and private investigator expertise of Ms. Virginia McDole. Without her steadfast efforts, it would have been extremely difficult to complete tasks such as the Hewett Family Tree on ancestry.com and the corresponding affidavits of heirships.

A special thank you is expressed to Mr. Herbert Lyles. Portrayed as *the friendly neighbor to the North*, of the Texas property, his encouragement and support of the family's efforts was invaluable.

Finally, I would like to acknowledge the support and guidance received from the following family members and friends; Anissa Turner, Rachelle Wilson, Robin Wilson, Taurian Shelvin, Martin Hewett, Jennifer Hewett, Jabari Griffin, Kyle Miller, Devin Pittman, Aron Pittman, Cara White, Walter Pittman III, and Robert Irving.

For without the assistance of the eyes, ears, and suggestions of all parties noted in the acknowledgments section, I might still be writing additional episodes to what could easily become an ongoing quest toward a clear pathway for the family legacy.

Musical Inspiration

Chapter One (Spotify Playlist 47)

I Want Jesus To Walk With Me – The Tabernacle Choir at Temple Square

Amazing Grace – London Philharmonic Choir

For Every Mountain – The Brooklyn Tabernacle Choir

Order My Steps – The Brooklyn Tabernacle Choir

How Great Thou Art – The Brooklyn Tabernacle Choir

Hallelujah You're Worthy – The Brooklyn Tabernacle Choir

Going Up Yonder – Walter Hawkins

The Lord's Prayer – Sheena Easton

It Is Well" (Instrumental) – Sam Levin (Sax For The Spirit)

If I Didn't Care – The Ink Spots

Chapter Three (Spotify Playlist 48)

Banana Boat (Day-O) - Harry Belafonte

(Artists) George Gershwin, Michael Tilson Thomas, Sarah Vaughan, Los Angeles Philharmonic (Medley)

But Not For Me

Love Is Here To Stay

Embraceable You

Someone To Watch Over Me

Fools Rush In (Where Angels Fear To Tread) – Billy Eckstine

Unforgettable - Nat King Cole

Only You (And You Alone) - The Platters

Face It Girl, It's Over – Nancy Wilson

Can't Take My Eyes Off You – Nancy Wilson

What the World Needs Now (Is Love) - Dionne Warwick

What a Wonderful World - Louis Armstrong

The Theme from a Summer Place - Percy Faith and His Orchestra

Chapter Six (Spotify Playlist 49)

Matilda - Harry Belafonte

Fly Me to the Moon - Sarah Vaughan

My Foolish Heart - Billy Eckstine

The Days of Wine and Roses – Billy Eckstine

When Sunny Gets Blue – Nat King Cole

Autumn Leaves – Nat King Cole

I Only Have Eyes for You – The Flamingos

Who Can I Turn To (When Nobody Needs Me) – Nancy Wilson

(You Don't Know) How Glad I am – Nancy Wilson

Walk on By – Dionne Warwick

Summertime (from Porgy & Bess) - Ella Fitzgerald, Louis Armstrong

Home - Stephanie Mills.

Photographic Images

Book Cover – Ron and Patty Thomas, *Molly Brook Cascades Through The Autumn Forest Near Groton Vermont*, Photography, iStock by Getty Images (ID: 108354929), www.istockphoto.com/photo/autumn-in-vermont-gm108354929-14277370

Figure A – LoveTheWind, *Group of people on peak mountain climbing helping team work , travel trekking success business concept*, Photography, iStock by Getty Images (ID: 1009803562, www.istockphoto.com/photo/group-of-people-on-peak-mountain-climbing-helping-team-work-travel-trekking-success-gm1009803562-272216359

Figure 1 – vicm, *white-tailed deer in forest in autumn*, Photography, iStock by Getty Images (ID: 182201866), www.istockphoto.com/photo/white-tailed-deer-gm182201866-11051727

Figure 2 – AVTG, *Sunbeams breaking through Spruce Tree Forest in autumn, rays of sunlight amongst trees and on moss covered forest floor*, Photography, iStock by Getty Images (ID: 499689946), www.istockphoto.com/photo/spruce-tree-forest-in-autumn-illuminated-by-sunbeams-through-fog-gm499689946-80368567

Figure 3 – vicm, *Large buck in forest*, Photography, iStock by Getty Images (ID: 175591253), www.istockphoto.com/photo/buck-in-forest-gm175591253-21244499

Figure 4 – Karel Bock, *Natural scene from Wisconsin state park*, Photography, iStock by Getty Images (ID: 1275868736), www.istockphoto.com/photo/the-young-white-tailed-deer-in-the-forest-gm1275868736-375859780

Figure 5 – magicflute002, *A vigorous, multi-flowering strain with several stems per bulb, fragrant Narcissus tazetta, creates lush, full display with two to twenty flowers with spreading petals per stout stem. Narcissus tazetta is also known as paperwhite, Narcissus, Jonquil and polyanthus narcissus*, Photography, iStock by Getty Images (ID: 1310895864), www.istockphoto.com/photo/narcissus-narcissus-tazetta-narcissus-tete-a-tete-gm1310895864-400151714

Figure 6 – Lara_Uhryn, *Amazing nature landscape with colored autumn forest and mountain creek, outdoor travel background suitable for wallpaper*, Photography, iStock by Getty Images (ID: 1335917843), www.istockphoto.com/photo/amazing-nature-landscape-with-colored-autumn-forest-and-mountain-creek-outdoor-gm1335917843-417386374

Figure 7 – Bkamprath, *Wild deer fawns in the beautiful Olympic National Park in Western Washington State USA*, Photography, iStock by Getty Images (ID: 1335424383), www.istockphoto.com/photo/wild-deer-fawns-in-the-beautiful-olympic-national-park-in-western-washington-state-gm1335424383-417162589

Figure 8 – RelaxFoto.de, *Autumn landscape with brook in forest*, Photography, iStock by Getty Images (ID: 92527579), www.istockphoto.com/photo/autumn-landscape-with-brook-in-forest-gm92527579-1138750

Figure 9 – FRANKHILDEBRAND, *Whitetail Deer Fawn*, Photography, iStock by Getty Images (ID: 147986101), www.istockphoto.com/photo/new-beginings-gm147986101-20745376

Figure 10 – Muhur, *A beautiful waterfall and autumn scene at Yedigoller National Park. Which is a famous national park at Bolu, Turkey.* Photography, iStock by Getty Images (ID: 502623815), www.istockphoto.com/photo/beautiful-waterfall-and-autumn-scene-at-yedigoller-gm502623815-43825912

Figure 11 – davemantel, *Family of deer in the woods in Sooke, BC.* Photography, iStock by Getty Images (ID: 1334896349), www.istockphoto.com/photo/deer-and-fawn-in-woods-gm1334896349-416840571

Figure 12 – Juan Paz, *table with glasses, flowers, cutlery, plants. Wedding decorations, table settings*, Photography, iStock by Getty Images (ID: 1395183633), www.istockphoto.com/photo/wedding-decoration-setting-table-gm1395183633-450388789

Contents

Chapter One

Who Am I?

I am the trajectory of a sphere,
Sent flying toward an ancestral foe.

I am the Rock of Ages
That withstood the shifting sands
And the foaming seas.

I am the synthetic product of four generations
Of de-educating, emasculating, and incorporating.

I am the genetic extension of the sons and daughters of Africa,
Usurped from their rightful homes as rulers of men.

I am the thankful recipient
Of the words, and deeds, of
Tubman, Dubois, Medgar, Malcolm, and Martin

I am the foreclosed mortgage
On a race riot, anti-poverty program, welfare check,
And educational system geared to a White-cultured society.

I am the mark of oppression
And the salvation fire
That burned the ropes on the hanging tree.

I am the voice of the four winds,
Rustling through the valleys of despair.

And I am the eternal life
That branded a white-hot message upon the midnight skies:

I am Black—and I am proud!

P*arents not including estate planning in occasional dinner table discussions could position their children for future legal problems.* 1955 I was eight years old and resided in Los Angeles, California. That was the year Florence Harris, my mother, first mentioned the fifty-six acres of undeveloped land in Shalene, Texas. I later learned that Shalene, Texas, is Henderson County's largest town and the county seat. It is conveniently located southeast of Dallas and north of Houston at the intersection of two major U.S. highways. The thick canopy of towering trees woven throughout the rugged East Texas terrain led to the emergence of the phrase Piney Woods Region.

On June 19, 1865 ("Juneteenth"), Union General Gordon Granger arrived in Galveston, Texas, and issued General Order Number 3. The Order read, "The people of Texas are informed that, in accordance with a proclamation from the Executive of the United States, all slaves are free. More specifically Order Number 3 proclaimed (a) an absolute equality of personal rights and rights of property between former masters and slaves, and (b) the connection heretofore existing between them became that between employer and hired labor. As such the freed were advised to remain at their present homes and work for wages."

On August 2, 1898, thirty-three years after the issuance of General Order Number 3, the deed to the Shalene, Texas property was recorded. The deed was from Sallie Simpson to Rosie Burse Edwards. Rosie was my great-grandmother. The granting of the land was instead of monetary compensation and represented repayment for services rendered by my family. Rosie Burse Edwards was born in February 1862. She passed away on December 24, 1919. After her death, the Shalene, Texas, property was passed on to all of her heirs. Rosie Edwards had eight children, so the resulting distribution of generational wealth, in the form of land, was quite extensive.

According to my mother, a major company had been slant-drilling oil from the property. As a result, royalty checks were sent to my mother and her siblings. I recall my mother being quite upset when the checks stopped coming. Citing declining oil reserve levels, the oil company determined drilling was no longer cost-effective. I also recall my mother being equally distressed by the actions of one of her second cousins. The family had left oversight of the small-town, rural Texas property to the cousin, who, in turn, abandoned the premises. She ran off to New York with a man and failed to inform anyone of her departure.

In 1986, the Pittman family sued Tommy Lee Wyatt for trespassing on the Shalene, Texas property. As a defense, Mr. Wyatt asserted a claim of adverse possession, which the court denied. Adverse possession refers to circumstances under which one may lawfully lay claim to ownership of property not originally one's own. Wyatt then provided the court with a deed. The signed, notarized deed stated that two "heirs of Rosie," as well as someone Mr. Wyatt claimed was also an "heir of Rosie," had sold the land to him.

The following family members were present during the 1986 Edwards/Pittman vs. Tommy Lee Wyatt court hearing: James Pittman (Uncle Jim), Maudell P. Williams (Aunt Maude), Anne P. Lilly (Aunt Anne), and Geraldine P. Wooten (Aunt Geri). In addition to the Pittman family attorney, the court appointed an attorney to represent the interests of the absent heirs. However, introducing the deed into evidence prompted a change of plans.

The Pittman attorney advised the family members to ask the judge to dismiss the jury and reach an out-of-court settlement. As part of the agreement, Tommy Lee Wyatt received 25.3 acres. Mr. Wyatt's attorney objected to the Pittman family attorney's request for a property division. Thirty-seven years have elapsed since the 1986 interlocutory judgment. A review of records conducted by a Houston, Texas-based law firm confirmed that from 1986 to 2023, steps to enforce a legal partition were not completed. As a result, the property was still listed in the Henderson County records as 56 acres of undivided interest.

Addressing the results of the 1986 hearing, Aunt Maude wrote a letter dated March 19, 1986, to "Dear Family Members."

"This letter is to inform you that our family <u>WON</u> the court case involving the property in Shalene, Texas. That's great, isn't it?!

"On Monday, March 3, 1986, Jim, Anne, and I went to Shalene, Texas, where Attorney Mary Daffin represented us. She was super! We drove up from Houston early Monday morning intending to be in court only <u>one</u> day. We ended up having to spend two nights and being in court 2½ days. After hearing both sides, Edwards/Pittman vs. Tommy Lee Wyatt, the Judge agreed that we indeed were the rightful heirs to this property. To the best of our ability, we answered questions on the stand and also entered into evidence a large notebook with old letters, receipts, and canceled checks proving our claim.

"The amount of land involved was 56 acres. We won all of that back but 3 parcels. Those were given to Tommy Lee Wyatt some time ago by Uncle Buddy (Green Edwards). That was my mother's brother. The other was given away by George Martin, Aunt Rebecca's son, and someone named Levi Jackson gave his part also to Tommy Lee Wyatt. So we get all but those 3 shares. After this land is surveyed, we'll know exactly how many acres we'll have proper and clear title to.

"The most important issue now that faces <u>all of us</u> is the payment of the attorneys. We are attaching the latest bill for your consideration:

"Amount Due: Attorney P. (old attorney) $700.00
                 Attorney D. (new Attorney) $4,156.18
                 TOTAL $4,856.18

"We expect another bill from a third attorney, from Shalene, Texas. He was hired by the court to represent the unknown heirs of the property. He, too, did a fantastic job in representing us in court. We must pay him, also.

"Since our attorney has done what we hired her to do, it is URGENT that we all share in this expense. We four here in Houston—Jim, Anne, Geraldine, and I—have done the leg work, and paperwork, and represented you in court, and in the attorneys' office. We cannot foot this bill alone. The property now belongs to all of us <u>equally</u>.

We realize times are tough and money is not easily available but we need to hear from each of you soon. If you have children or grandchildren, ask them to contribute something, too. They, too, are heirs.

"As usual checks or money orders may be made payable to: MAUDELL Williams. We will then deposit it in the special account and pay the attorneys. We have the bill, and they expect to be paid!

"The attached map shows the property that is ours now. As you notice, there is no <u>access road</u> to the acreage. The only way in is through someone else's land. We still have never seen the property. It may be necessary to have roads built.

"We hope this letter has not been too long, but wanted you to know of our happiness and success, and to ask you to send your money, right away, <u>as much</u> as possible.

Thank you. Urgently yours, Maude, Anne, Jim, and Geraldine."

The term "heirs' property" applies to the scenario linked to the 56 acres of undivided interest in Shalene, Texas. A summary of Texas law, as it pertains to heirs' property, is shown below (*Heirs' Property: Understanding the Legal Issues in Texas* by Francine Miller, November 2022; see Appendixes for additional information about heirs' property).

- Heirs' property (sometimes known as family land) is a property that has been transferred to multiple family members by inheritance, usually without a will. Typically, it is created when land is transferred from someone who dies without a will to that person's spouse, children, or other heirs who have a legal right to the property.
- When heirs' property is created, the heirs own all the property together (in legal terms, they own the property as "tenants in common"). In other words, they each own an interest in the undivided land rather than each heir owning an individual lot or piece of the land.
- In addition to the above, unless the heirs go to the appropriate administrative agency or court in their jurisdiction and have the

title or deed to the land changed to reflect their ownership, the land will remain in the name of the person who died.

- To resolve heirs' property issues, an important first step is tracing the ownership of the land from the original titled owner to the current owners. Many practitioners encourage heirs' property owners to build a family tree identifying all the heirs, deceased and living.

- When a person dies with a valid will, they die "testate," and their will determines who inherits their property. When a person dies without a will, they die "intestate," and state law governing intestate succession determines who inherits that person's real estate and other assets. Who inherits a person's land by intestate succession varies depending on which family members survive the decedent.

- The Uniform Partition of Heirs' Property Act (UPHPA) is codified in the Texas Property Code, Title 4, Chapter 23A. The UPHPA allows co-owners in possession of heirs' property to partition the property by sale if it cannot be partitioned in kind. A partition by sale results when the property cannot be easily divided into equal parts.

George Santayana was born on December 16, 1863, and passed away on September 26, 1952. He was a philosopher, essayist, poet, and novelist and is often credited with the famous quote, "Those who cannot remember the past are doomed to repeat it." Santayana's quote assists in highlighting a key issue linked to the Shalene, Texas, property. About it, the issue was a tendency on the part of bordering neighbors to lay claim to the property.

Aunt Maude's letter provided the next generation with a cornerstone to build. Clues provided in the letter, when combined, would later serve as an anchor amid a stormy sea. These invaluable clues also highlighted the myriad problems linked to the property. The goal of the descendants of Rosie was to chart a strategy to address an ongoing concern that had been lingering for decades. Similar to a technique used by firefighters, some clues served as fire line safety nets. Like pearls of wisdom sprinkled along the way, these clues were passed from generation to generation, in writing as well as by word of mouth. However, when it came to implementing a future course of action, not all clues had the same impact. This fact underscored the need to prioritize clues linked to topics such as sell versus partition.

Similarities emerged when comparing the Shalene, Texas, dilemma and the jigsaw puzzle approach often employed by crime scene detectives. By definition, a jigsaw puzzle is any set of varied, irregularly shaped pieces. When these pieces were properly assembled, they formed a picture or a map. In Henderson County, the four parcels of heirs' property were displayed on a Henderson County plat map. The map also included a fifth parcel which represented the 25.3 acres that were relinquished to the encroaching neighbor in 1986. The steps used by Sherlock Holmes could be of assistance in addressing the Shalene predicament.

Sherlock Holmes, a fictional character created by British writer Arthur Conan Doyle, has emerged as a model for the contemporary mastermind detective. Identifying himself as the world's first and only "consulting detective," Holmes first appeared in Conan Doyle's *A Study in Scarlet* (published in Beeton's *Christmas Annual* of 1887).

Dr. Watson is Holmes's best friend, assistant, and flatmate. As the biographer/historian of Sherlock Holmes, Watson is the narrator of all of the stories in *The Adventures of Sherlock Holmes*. He is also the narrator for many of the forty-eight other stories featuring these characters that are not in the first collection of twelve.

In contrast to the more eccentric Holmes, Watson is described as a classic Victorian-era gentleman. Holmes rebuffed praise that declared his abilities to be "elementary." The oft-quoted phrase, "Elementary, my dear Watson," never actually appeared in Conan Doyle's writings. However, Holmes did offer some insight into his method by claiming "When you have excluded the impossible, whatever remains, however improbable, must be the truth."

Danielle K. Kincaid wrote an article titled "The Sherlock Holmes Conundrum, or The Difference Between Deductive and Inductive Reasoning" (Feb 17, 2015). According to Ms. Kincaid, although

Sherlock Holmes incorporated other types of reasoning, he primarily used inductive reasoning. The latter approach allowed him to observe a crime scene or other scenario, and then use his observations to arrive at a plausible conclusion about events that had not yet been observed. In sum, inductive reasoning can be defined as a method of concluding by going from the specific to the general.

According to Sadia Maqsood, writer, editor, and blogger, "The point of thinking like a detective is to be able to make better judgments, to predict things ahead of time, to come up with practical solutions to everyday problems, and to keep your brain's creative machinery running," S. Maqsood, "5 Genius Tricks For Problem-Solving From the Famous Sherlock Holmes," May 30, 2021; https://medium.com/mind-cafe/how-to-think-like-sherlock-holmes-47c125e40ad9. Ms. Maqsood used the following keywords as headings for a discussion of tricks and techniques linked to the process of thinking like Sherlock Holmes:

1. Think backward
2. Disengage from the task
3. Always be a skeptic
4. Eliminate the inessential and
5. Observe – but not just with the eye

In addition to the above, Ms. Maqsood stated, "To begin observing like Sherlock Holmes, follow these steps.
1. Engage all senses: sight, hearing, taste, touch, and smell.
2. Notice the finer details, not just the glaringly obvious.
3. Connect the dots. Connect observation A to observation B to observation C and so on, and
4. Identify patterns. What are recurring themes, things keep repeating themselves?"

Sadia Maqsood also noted that adherence to the latter steps would enable the researcher to come up with a testable hypothesis and make predictions instead of jumping to conclusions without evidence.

The following passage reveals quite a few relevant clues:

Addressing the results of the 1986 hearing, Aunt Maude wrote a letter dated March 19, 1986, to "Dear Family Members":

"This letter is to inform you that our family <u>WON</u> the court case involving the property in Shalene, Texas. That's great, isn't it?"

Clue: According to Aunt Maude, "The amount of land involved was 56 acres. We won all of that back but 3 parcels. Those were given to Tommy Lee Wyatt some time ago by Uncle Buddy (Green Edwards). That was my mother's brother. The other was given away by George Martin, Aunt Rebecca's son, and someone named Levi Jackson gave his part also to Tommy Lee Wyatt. So we get all but those 3 shares. After this land is surveyed, we'll know exactly how many acres we'll have proper and clear title to" (think backward)

Clue: "And someone named Levi Jackson," implies that Aunt Maude was not convinced that Levi Jackson was an actual family heir (always be a skeptic)

Clue: Aunt Maude reached out to the entire family for assistance in collectively shouldering the property's financial burden (think backward)

Clue: There was no access road to the acreage. The only way in was through someone else's land (think backward)

Clue: The aunts and uncle ("the elders") had never seen the property (think backward)

Similar to their predecessors, the Twenty-First-century generation of first cousins (Connye, Judlyne, Jimmy, and Darilyn) had not visited the property. That is, except Connye, who once visited the property along with Cody James. Cody James is a Shalene, Texas attorney who specializes in real estate. Cody James purchased the heirs' former 25.3 acres from Annie Wyatt (widow of the late Tommy Lee Wyatt). The 2013 meeting between Connye and Cody James took place in Shalene, Texas.

According to Connye, Cody James invited her to view the Shalene property. However, the tour stopped short of actually walking through the land. Instead, the attorney escorted Connye to a gate in a neighbor's yard. He then pointed off into the distance toward a cluster of dense brush and heavy vegetation and said, "And out there is your property."

After the 2013 meeting, Cody James threatened to file a lawsuit against the heirs of Rosie. The goal of the lawsuit was to force the heirs to sell the 30.8 acres to him for $400 per acre. At the time, a rumor was circulating in Shalene that a major poultry company would be coming to town. The company was seeking grazing land in town. However, there was a catch: the company would only consider parcels of 50 acres or more.

Similar to the transfer of a baton during a relay race, the elders passed on to the next generation the responsibility for payment of annual property taxes. The property was landlocked and there were no easement rights, the next generation was tasked with identifying an easement path as well as securing a partition.

Clue: Landlocked
- A parcel of land (lot) is landlocked (enclaved) if it has no access to the public road or if this access is insufficient, difficult, or impassable.
- Public roads include not only provincial and municipal streets and roads, but also any road leading to them.
- As such, an easement across Ms. Delgado's property is necessary to access the Harris family's land and is supported by facts and in law (think backward)

Clue: Easement (See Appendixes for additional information about easements)

- An easement is a means by which a landowner grants another person the right to use the landowner's property for a specific purpose. The land on which the easement is granted is referred to as the servient estate, and the land the easement benefits is referred to as the dominant estate (think backward)
- A property owner cannot block an easement if it was already mentioned in the property's deed. If the property owner attempts to contest the easement's boundaries, a property survey is warranted (think backward)
- An express easement is the most common type that an individual or entity can obtain. The latter easement can be structured via a grant or reservation. When an express easement is granted, the landowner provides another party with the ability to use their land for right-of-way purposes (think backward)

Clue: Connye's interactions with Cody James would later emerge as a possible option in a future lawsuit. According to the Henderson County Assessor's Office, the property was viewed as 56 acres of undivided interest. Therefore, a future legal strategy might be to force the sale of all 56 acres (think backward)

Clue: Like their predecessors, the Twenty-First- century generation of first cousins had not visited the Shalene, Texas, property except Connye, who once viewed the property from a distance, accompanied by attorney Cody James (think backward)

The previous generation of sisters (and one brother) consisted of James L. Pittman Sr. (Uncle Jim), Maudell P. Williams (Aunt Maude), Anne P. Lilly (Aunt Anne), and Geraldine P. Wooten (Aunt Geri).

The Houston, Texas–based group of siblings was quite cohesive. For many decades, my aunts and uncle sang together in the Pilgrim Congregational Church Choir.

I can only imagine the joy my aunts and uncle must have shared as they harmonized with African spiritual hymns such as "I Want Jesus To Walk With Me." In addition, they probably sang Christian hymns like "Amazing Grace," "For Every Mountain," "Order My Steps," 'How Great Thou Art," "Hallelujah You're Worthy," and "Going Up Yonder."

The latter song was generally associated with usher boards/choir entry/exits and collection plate scenarios. During the annual Christmas services, I suspect they also sang the central Christian prayer, "The Lord's Prayer." Perhaps there were instrumental versions like "It Is Well," designed to persuade new members to walk down the aisle and join the church.

Along with sharing their deep spiritual beliefs, my aunts and uncles helped to shape and develop several aspects of my worldview. My mother Florence, sister to Maude, Anne, Geraldine, and James, came from a large family comprised of five girls and six boys. The Pittman family home was located on Bringhurst Street in Houston's Fifth Ward. Of this group, Foster Pittman (Uncle Brother), Robert Pittman (Uncle Bobby), and Walter Pittman (Uncle Abbey) migrated from Houston to the Los Angeles, California, area.

The term "mitiblende" was once used in 1964 at the beginning of my senior year in high school. I came home and encountered a burglar in the apartment. The series of events that led up to the use of the term are shown below;

The school day concluded and I had just walked the final leg of the two-mile stretch home. Upon my arrival at the Towne Avenue address, I traversed the long driveway that stretched behind the residential property and climbed the stairs to our apartment. As soon as I reached the front door, it was clear that something was wrong. One of the glass wings in the louver window next to the door had been broken. I turned the knob to the right and discovered that the door was unlocked. I opened it and entered the living room. To my surprise,

13

a man was sitting on the couch with his back to the large picture window. He was wearing a brown sports coat and black slacks.

"Who are you?" I asked

"I am an old friend of your mother from Houston. My name is John – John Smith."

Observing the broken glass on the floor, I said, "It looks like someone broke in here."

"Yeah, Sherman. I arrived a short while ago, and your mother was upset about the break-in. However, she had to leave for a beauty shop appointment and asked me to stay here until she returned."

I was puzzled because one of the last things my mother had said to me before I departed for TJH (an abbreviation for my high school) that morning was that she had a beauty shop appointment. She was a single mom, and she had the occasional male visitor. However, leaving a strange man in the house – without a proper introduction to the family – was something she would never do. Confounding matters, this particular stranger seemed to be aware that my family had roots in Houston, Texas.

The plot thickened when John, as he called himself, kept referring to me as Sherman. Sherman wasn't my name. My impression was that he was a little high on something. The parts of John's story that didn't add up outweighed the parts that did, but there was just enough to make his story halfway believable. However, if this man was a burglar and had harmed my mother, I fully intended to do my best to put a serious hurt on him.

I took a few steps toward the hallway that led to the bathroom and the adjacent bedrooms and glanced around. I noticed fragments of my sister Lynette's broken piggy bank on the floor. It didn't help that John, who stood about six foot two and looked like he weighed about 190 pounds, got up from the couch and followed me into the hallway. For a brief moment, I had my back to him. At that point, he could have easily gotten the drop on me and taken me out.

I pointed to the piggy bank fragments on the floor. "That's my sister's piggy bank."

"Yes, it appears that someone took some money from the piggy bank."

A sixth sense told me not to continue deeper into the bedroom area. The kitchen to my right had a sliding door that led to a small utility porch with a double-sink basin.

I turned to John and said, "You know what, I forgot something downstairs. I'll be right back."

John shrugged and stepped aside to let me pass. I exited the apartment and hastily scampered down the stairs. Upon reaching the driveway, I began to jog toward the landlord's residence. On the sidewalk, I accelerated into a hundred-meter top-end sprint speed toward the beauty shop at the end of the block. I entered the shop, probably looking a little wild-eyed and sweating profusely. I did my best to calm down as I approached my mother.

"Hi, Joe," my mother said with a smile. She was sitting under one of the dryers.

As calmly as I could, I asked, "Mom, did you leave a man sitting in the living room?"

Her look of shock and dismay answered my question. "What man!" she shouted.

Similar to the cartoons I used to watch when I was much younger, I felt like a big neon sign had just appeared over my head spelling out "Sucker!" *I'd been played! The only thing missing from this picture was the TJH marching band!* Without uttering another word, I nodded toward my mother, exited the beauty shop, and began sprinting back to the apartment.

Clearing the long driveway, I scrambled up the stairs and opened the door. To my surprise, John—or whatever his name was—was still there. He was unscrewing the legs from the stereo hi-fi unit.

I confronted him. "You lied to me. Who the hell are you!"

John mumbled something and—seemingly empty-handed walked toward the front door. He exited the apartment and proceeded down the stairs.

Halfway down, John was confronted by my mother. She said, "Mister, who are you?" She was accompanied by the landlord's wife and the lady who lived downstairs.

I had often observed my mother privately styling her own hair and was used to seeing her in the kitchen with a hot comb steaming on one of the stove burners. I was still surprised by her appearance that day. It seemed to me that she was the inventor of the natural hairstyle. Like me, my mother had a smooth ebony complexion and narrow lips. She was still wearing the white smock from the beauty shop, and her hair flared out in all directions.

The unexpected visual of my five-foot-four mom in her full-blown Afro glory prompted John to pause. After he regained his composure, John started to mumble to himself and continued until he reached the end of the stairway. He made an abrupt right turn and started walking toward the rear of the apartment complex, where he encountered a six-foot cement block wall, John hoisted himself up and over the wall and down into Lee's (a TJH classmate) backyard.

I followed and tried futilely to get him to come back. My commands fell on deaf ears. To my mother's dismay, I turned around, gave her a wink, hoisted myself up over the wall, and continued my pursuit of John. I heard my mother pleading for me to come back, but I felt like I had an obligation to handle the situation. Unfortunately, it appeared that Lee wasn't home. If reinforcements weren't available, I was on my own. It would have helped if Lee had a vicious pit bull roaming the yard, but that was not the case.

I continued to follow John north up Crocker Avenue toward East Vernon. Despite my persistent urgings, John was not coming back. I followed him across East Vernon and into an alley that stretched east toward Avalon. Halfway through the alley, it became clear that my efforts to persuade John to return to the Towne Avenue location had failed. His only response to my frequent requests was, "Sherman, what you following me for? You need to get on back home."

At that point, I realized I was too deep in the alley for comfort. I paused long enough to pick up an empty Purex bottle. I tried to hide the dark-brown glass bottle behind my back, grasping it tightly in my right hand, and continued to follow John.

I was five foot eleven and weighed 135, and John was six foot two and 190. It was clear that I was a lightweight. Short of mixed martial arts training, which I did not have, the only ammunition at my disposal was that empty Purex bottle.

Glancing back at me, John noticed that I had one arm behind my back. He stopped, turned toward me with a scowl on his face, and said, "Sherman, what you got there behind your back?"

"I asked you to come on back!" I replied defiantly.

John reached into his pocket, pulled out a pocketknife, and unlocked the blade.

In retrospect, I see the comparisons between my 1964 alley encounter and the attempted mugging of Nick in the 1986 comedy *Crocodile Dundee*. In response to the perp's demand for his wallet, Nick said, "That's not a knife. That's a *knife!*"

We began to circle each other, and I knew I only had one move left. I hurled the bottle with as much force as possible, hoping to make contact with John's face and jam his control tower. However, my aim was altered by nervous tension, and the Purex bottle ended up shattering against his chest.

John took one step backward and shouted, "Ow! God damn you, Sherman!"

The blunt force of the bottle ricocheting off his chest had served its purpose. It provided the shock value I needed to execute a reverse pivot maneuver. I combined that move with what can best be described as a Roadrunner windup, followed by a shot out of the cannon, and a hundred-meter top-end sprint down the alley.

Probably the only thought running through my mind was, *If this jive turkey catches me from behind, maybe I deserve to be cut!*

After exiting from the alley, I slowed to a jog and headed towards the Towne Avenue apartment. When I informed my mother of the altercation she said, "Joe, you got to learn how to mitiblende! I didn't like any of that—that man could have hurt you."

I just shrugged. I was familiar with the term. "Mitiblende" was a word coined by Uncle Bobby, who once sang tenor for The Ink Spots. Among other melodic contributions, he provided the vocals for the hit song "If I Didn't Care." When Uncle Bobby used the term mitiblende, he meant make the brains grow smarter.

Long before my teenage encounter with the term, I experienced a mitiblende moment with Uncle Bobby. I was just five years old at the time. Uncle Bobby was driving my family from the Rose Hills Projects to a new home on the east side of Los Angeles. Uncle Abbey also traveled with us and assisted with the moving process. The owner of the 48th Street rental was the aunt of a female singer Uncle Bobby had befriended while navigating the rhythm and blues entertainment network.

In 1952, at age five, many would have described me as a spirited, rather spunky child with a penchant for adventure. Back then, Uncle Bobby drove a 1937 avocado-green, four-door Oldsmobile. The rear door of the vehicle was secured by a piece of white bed sheet that had been tied into a knot. Similar to most siblings, there was a scramble for dibs on a back seat with a window view. Both Rowena and Lynette, my sisters, were older and taller than me, so the luck of the draw yielded the seat adjacent to the compromised door for me. Before my family departed from the Rose Hills Projects, I recall Uncle Bobby shouting instructions to the back seat occupants: "Whatever you do, do not lean against that door!"

The route Uncle Bobby selected took us over the Los Angeles River. My inquisitive nature led me to lean on the door, ever so slightly, just to see if there was water in the river. That's when the car door swung open and took me with it. The vehicle was moving about 50 mph, so I was left clinging to the door and swinging in midair. I did my best to keep my legs bent upward so that my feet wouldn't scrap the fast-moving asphalt below. It took all the stamina I could muster just to hold on. Probably because I was in shock, I couldn't come up with the extra strength needed to utter a sound.

There I was with my five-year-old derriere hanging out, all undignified-like, over the Los Angeles River and dangling in the breeze while simultaneously experiencing successive waves of embarrassment and humiliation. By my account, the temporarily suspended animation seemed to last an eternity. In those fleeting seconds, a movie of my entire life flashed before my eyes. Although the LA River episode didn't have a rags-to-riches ending, the movie could have been nominated for an Academy Award in the short film category.

During the initial part of the journey, both sisters next to me were gazing out the opposite window. However, as the drama unfolded, Uncle Bobby must have glanced in the rearview mirror, because he shouted, "I told you not to lean against that door!" He decelerated and pulled over to the side of the bridge. Once the vehicle had rolled to a stop, I was able to scamper back into the car.

And just like that, my window-view privileges were revoked for the remainder of the trip. There I sat, sandwiched between Rowena and Lynette, feeling dejected and humiliated. The same sisters who, to the delight of the cheering Rose Hills crowd, shouted, "That's not the way you eat at home!" during the playground pie eating contest. The thing was, with both hands tied behind my back, I hadn't bargained on the whipped cream and vanilla pudding pie going up my nostrils.

Years later, Aunt Geri would tell me, "Well, that's just the way it is between brothers and sisters; you are not going to get a lot of positive feedback from your sisters."

As a result of my up close and personal encounter with the Los Angeles River, the joy I felt at the beginning of the pilgrimage had just about been extinguished. However, the excitement was rekindled when we reached our destination and began exploring the two-story, four-bedroom-plus-den home. The dwelling was spacious, in comparison to the compact two-bedroom, upstairs/downstairs Rose Hills unit. The new home even had a room adjacent to the attic. Of course, Rowena and Lynette immediately called dibs on that space as their girls-only bedroom. There was also an enclosed front porch area, adjacent to the guest bedroom. The porch area turned out to be a perfect fit for the boys-only-room bunk beds.

Chapter Two

It has been sixty-nine years since the 1952 Los Angeles River incident and fifty-eight years since an unwelcome intruder breached the family apartment in 1964. A brief summary of events that occurred since 1952 is shown below;

1965 Graduated Valedictorian from Thomas Jefferson High School, L.A. CA

1969 Graduated from the First Private College of Clareville, California with a B.A. degree in Psychology, Clareville, CA

1969 Accepted into three medical schools. Selected a Special Five-Year Program for Disadvantaged Minorities at WWLA's School of Medicine, L.A. CA. I was enrolled in the medical school from 1969 to 1971. However, for several reasons, only one of the four minority students enrolled completed the program.

1972 Graduated from WWLA's Graduate School of Public Health with an M.P.H. degree in Health Administration, L.A. CA

1982 Graduated from the First Southern University of Los Angeles, California with a Ph.D. and M.P.A. in Public Administration

In addition to the above, I held the following positions from 1972 (the beginning of my full-time work-life) to the present;

- President of J.H. Consultants, Inc., Inglewood, California
- Online and Classroom faculty for a national university (1996 – 2024), Phoenix, Arizona
- Director of Research/MIS & Grants Writer for a community college, Compton, California
- Program Specialist/Training Unit for a police department, Inglewood, California
- Evaluation Consultant, The United Way, Los Angeles, California
- Field Operations Supervisor (Quality Assurance), The United States Bureau of the Census, Inglewood, California
- Assistant to the Vice President of Academic Affairs/Evaluation Specialist, for a historically Black medical university, Los Angeles, California
- Research Analyst, for a local health department, Los Angeles, California
- Teaching Assistant/Research Assistant for a private university, Los Angeles, California
- Research Associate Consultant, for a grant-funded program, Los Angeles, California
- Associate Director of Finances, for a local family planning program, Los Angeles, California and
- Assistant Marketing Director, for a local prepaid health plan, Los Angeles, California

In 2013, at age sixty-five, I was invited to join four first cousins in paying the annual taxes on the Shalene, Texas, property. However, differences of opinion sometimes emerged between the first cousins regarding future courses of action.

Reflecting upon concepts such as the transfer of generational wealth, I recall thinking, *Similar to me, my first cousins are gradually approaching their golden years and simply have other priorities.*

A summary of how I became involved with the property is as follows:

- In 2013, a first cousin requested assistance in paying Geraldine Pittman Wooten's taxes. I agreed to make the payment.
- In 2013, Cody James, a Shalene, Texas, attorney, threatened to file a lawsuit against the Heirs of Rosie. His goal was to force the family to sell the remaining 30.8 acres to him for $400 an acre.
- The first cousins asked me to locate an attorney who would defend the family against the possible lawsuit.
- The attorney I selected was licensed to practice real estate law in Florida, Oklahoma, and Texas.
- The latter attorney provided the first cousins with a plan to purchase the 25.3 acres the family lost as part of a 1986 interlocutory judgment. The cost of the proposed purchase would be $400 an acre.
- Unfortunately, the first cousins were not in favor of the attorney I selected.
- The first cousins were opposed to the fact that he resided in Florida.
- The first cousins also preferred to sell the Shalene, Texas, land as opposed to buying additional property.
- In addition, the first cousins decided to release me from participating in the Shalene, Texas, process because I did not reside in Texas.
- The first cousins then retained the services of a local attorney from a Northeast Texas city.

- The Northeast Texas attorney did not meet the expectations of my first cousins.
- In 2018, one of my first cousins called me and requested additional assistance in paying Aunt Geri's back taxes. At the time, Aunt Geri was residing in a nursing home. The first cousin expressed concern that my aunt's daughter may have stopped making the annual payments. I contacted the Henderson County Tax Assessor's Office. A representative confirmed that Aunt Geri's taxes were in arrears. I promptly paid the past-due taxes.
- However, this time I informed my first cousins that I planned to structure a general warranty deed, which would allow me to assume the place of Aunt Geri on the county tax rolls.

Clue: The attorney, based in a city near the Florida Panhandle, provided the family with a plan to purchase the 25.3 acres that my aunts and uncle were advised by legal counsel to give away in 1986. The cost of the proposed purchase would be $400 an acre (think backward)

Clue: Although not selected to represent the heirs, the Florida Panhandle attorney took a special interest in the family's progress toward addressing the Shalene, Texas, situation. He often shared words of wisdom and encouragement, at timely intervals, along the way (think backward)

March 19, 2018:
Letter from Joe Harris to Isabella Delgado

Dear Ms. Delgado,

I am contacting you to see if you would be interested in purchasing my family's 30.8-acre property in Shalene, Texas. I believe the parcel numbers for the family properties are: (four (4) parcel numbers for the 30.8 acres).

Among other property holdings, it is my understanding that you own the Parcel number (parcel number for the 25.2 acres). On the

Henderson plat map the combination of my family's 30.8 acres and your 25.2 acres shows 56 acres of undivided interest.

According to the Platt map my family's property is bordered as follows: (1) on the West by Annie Wyatt (60 acres), (2) on the East by Isabella Delgado (90 acres), (3) on the North by Edward and Elaine Fontenette (33 acres), (4) on the South by Isabella Delgado (5 acres), and (5) on the South by an underground Texas oil or gas pipeline (probably inactive).

The legal description for the parcel number (tract number) is shown below.

(legal description of the property)

The assessed value for each of my family's parcels is $10,504. So, the total assessed value for the 30.8 acres is $42,012. According to the Henderson Assessor's Office, 31 acres of similarly situated properties in the Sanchez School District (our property is located in the Sanchez School District) sold in 2016 for (1) $62,264 (31 acres) and (2) $72,300 (31 acres).

If you are interested in purchasing our 30.8-acre property, please contact me as soon as possible.

April 2, 2018,
Edward Fontenette Called re: March 23, 2018, Certified Letter

The conversation was friendly and cordial. However, he was not interested in purchasing the Shalene, Texas, property at that time.

April 19, 2018
Telephone Call from Isabella Delgado in Response to a Certified Letter Dated March 19, 2018, and a Message Left on Her Landline

During the April 19, 2018, teleconference initiated by Ms. Delgado, the following exchange occurred:

"Ms. Delgado this property has been in my family since 1898, why are you interested in our land?" I asked

"I want the property for my children," she replied.

"Ms. Delgado, how much did you pay for my family's 25.3 acres?" I continued.

25

"Well, I don't rightly recollect, are the taxes current on your 30.8 acres?" she answered.

"Yes, the taxes are current. Ms. Delgado, you wouldn't like it if you had to ask for someone's permission to visit your property," I continued.

" No, I would not," she replied.

"Ms. Delgado, is there a road leading to our property that stretches across the 5-acre strip to the south?"

"Yes, there is a road."

"Ms. Delgado, are you an attorney?" I asked.

"No, are you?" she countered.

"No, I am not. I have a PhD in Public Administration," I replied.

"A PhD! Well, that makes you smarter than an attorney!" she surmised.

> **Clue:** A review of Ms. Delgado's past activity revealed a rather troubling pattern. Ms. Delgado's purchase of 90 acres of land to the east (2006), 25.2 acres of land to the north (2014), and 5 acres of land to the south (2014) effectively landlocked the Harris Family's property. In general, the majority of the first cousins were not pleased with the pattern of behavior she displayed in attempting to acquire the property. In addition, her responses to many of my questions appeared to be lacking in openness and sincerity (always be a skeptic)

April 19, 2018:
Email from Joe Harris to Isabella Delgado

Me: Good evening, Ms. Delgado, I am pleased that you are still interested in purchasing the Shalene property. It has come to my attention that there are deer hunting stations + deer feeding stations on the 25.2 acres that formerly belonged to my family. I assume you have leased the land out and are generating revenue from the deer hunting activity. Have you constructed a secure fence or border between your 25.2 acres and our remaining 30.8 acres? If not, then I suspect that the deer hunters have been roaming freely throughout our property without our consent. So far, my family has not been contacted regarding the sharing of any revenue generated from the deer hunting activity. I remain optimistic that we can come to a reasonable agreement regarding the proposed selling price of our 30.8 acres.

April 19, 2018:
Table 1 - Confirmed Sales to Isabella Delgado

Category (vacant land) Henderson County Appraisal District	Per Partial Value	30.8-acre Value (vacant land)	Per Acre Value
Assessed Value	$10,503	$42,012	$1,364.03
2016 Confirmed Sale		$103,425 (29.51-acres)	$3,504.74
2016 Confirmed Sale		$88,102 (30.38 -acres)	$2,900
2016 Confirmed Sale		$72,300	$2,332.26
2016 Confirmed Sale		$62,264	$2,008.52
Average Value (confirmed sales only)			$2,686.38
Suggested asking Price:	30.38 x $2,686.38	= $82,740.50	

> **Clue:** A review of confirmed sales reveals that the average selling price for 30.8 acres of vacant land was $82,740.50 or $2,686.38 per acre (think backward)

April 20, 2018:
Summary of Email from Isabella Delgado to Joe Harris

Isabella Delgado: She thanked me for reaching out to her and indicated that at this time she had no interest in purchasing the property at the price points I had suggested.

> **Clue:** Ms. Delgado not only declined to respond to the direct questions I asked about the deer hunting operation but withdrew her interest in purchasing the property (Observe—but not just with the eye)

April 20, 2018:
Email from Joe Harris to Isabella Delgado

Me: Good afternoon, Ms. Delgado, just a note to confirm receipt of your email. Yesterday, during the teleconference, you initiated you asked me to send you the four (4) closed values for comparable sales in 2016—And I complied with your request. You also asked me to provide you with the source of my confirmed sales information—I complied with your request. As I had to depart for a dental appointment, it was my understanding that you were going to call me today for a follow-up teleconference. It was also my understanding that, during the follow-up teleconference, you were going to provide the price point that you were willing to offer. A major point of disagreement in yesterday's brief teleconference was that—from your perspective our property was landlocked—and the expressed values should be those for landlocked properties. However, from my perspective, you have access to our property from the North, East, and South. This means that for an outside bidder, the property is indeed landlocked— However, for you, it is not landlocked. It is my understanding that our property became landlocked as a result of two (2) simultaneous purchases that you made in 2014. One of those purchases was for our family's former 25.2 acres (to the north), the other for a five-acre strip to the south. You already own the 90 acres that border our property on the east. Instead, of providing me with the expected counteroffer, it appears that you have elected to completely withdraw your expressed decision to purchase the property. Have I correctly interpreted the email correspondence that you sent today?

April 20, 2018:
Follow-up Email from Joe Harris to Isabella Delgado

Me: Good afternoon Ms. Delgado, there was something that I was prepared to discuss with you during the anticipated follow-up telephone call (that did not take place). At any rate, I forgot to mention this concept in the email that was sent to you earlier today If personal finances are one of your concerns, I am prepared to offer you a payment schedule. Step 1—Some sort of agreement on an asking price. Step 2—Some sort of agreement on a fixed term (e.g. 5 years or 10 years etc.). Step 3—Some sort of agreement on an interest rate. In sum, you would own the property, pay taxes on the property, and be required to make monthly payments to my family. Please let me know if the amortization schedule I am referencing would be something you would be interested in

April 23, 2018:
Summary of Email from Isabella Delgado to Joe Harris

Isabella Delgado: Ms. Delgado indicated that she would be willing to pay $400.00 per acre for the Harris family's property and noted that the latter value calculates to an all-cash offer of $12,320 for the 30.8 acres.

> **Clue:** The extremely low value of $400/acre matched the dollar amount Attorney   Cody James had previously offered my first cousin Connye (think backward)

> **Clue:** The initial $400/acre, later followed by $800/acre low-ball offers painted Ms. Delgado as someone who didn't have the best interest of my family in mind. In this Catch-22 scenario, Ms. Delgado justified her lowball offers by stating that the dollar amounts were based upon the landlocked rate (always be a skeptic)

On April 25, 2018, I contacted a Shalene, Texas-based real estate agent. After I provided a summary of the issues associated with the property, the agent asked, "At what point will y'all consider getting y'all selves an attorney?"

The agent then provided me with the name of a Shalene-based real estate attorney and said, "Perhaps the attorney could refer you to someone who could be of assistance."

Upon contacting the real estate agent I received the following

29

advice: "You are going to have to obtain an *easement* to sell the property," and "No realtor is going to take the listing without being able to see the property."

I followed the real estate agent's lead and initiated teleconferences with four Shalene attorneys.

I called the first attorney on April 25, 2018. I also sent an email to his secretary. A summary of the response received is as follows;

- (name of attorney) recommends that you contact (names and telephone numbers of two attorneys)
- Either attorney would be better suited to handle this type of situation for you

I received a call back from the second attorney on April 27, 2018. After introducing himself and asking a few preliminary questions, he stated "All of this is just one big mess! Ms. Delgado is rich. She owns a Chipotle Mexican Grill franchise in a neighboring city and has two attorneys she uses who work for her. Your best bet is to sell it to somebody next to you. Someone who will offer you an amount that is closer to the fair market value. Or find somebody who will sell you the easement rights. Essentially I am talking about going through the paperwork to determine (a) implied easement in the chain of title or (b) direct easement in the chain of title. Or to see if there are grounds in the paperwork for an easement by necessity. My retainer would be $15,000. The whole thing could easily run $20,000. So it's not worth it! Now you have a good day, you hear?"

As he was hanging up, I heard him laugh and mutter, "Why that shrewd old lady!"

Clue: As he was hanging up, I heard him laugh and mutter, "Why that shrewd old lady!" (engage all senses: hearing)

Clue: A future legal strategy might include: going through the paperwork to determine implied easement in the chain of title, direct easement in the chain of title, or seeing if there were grounds for an easement by necessity. (Connect the dots. Connect observation A to observation B to observation C and so on)

I spoke with the third attorney on April 30, 2018. After providing him with a brief overview of the situation he responded, "This doesn't sound like something I would handle. I don't do litigation. I just proceed forward once an easement has been granted." He then referred me to a fourth attorney.

I sent a letter dated April 30, 2018, to the fourth attorney. I then made a follow-up call to him on May 1, 2018. I received the following response from his secretary: "Yes, we did receive your letter. The attorney has been busy. It seems like he is always in court. Have you considered contacting other attorneys?"

The receptionist listened attentively as I underscored the urgency of my need for assistance. She also confirmed that she knew Annie Wyatt. Then she stated, "I will relay the information to the attorney and he will get back to you."

I assumed he would call me back if he was interested in the case. However, because I did not receive a callback, I concluded that he was not interested.

Prior to the April 2018 teleconference with the real estate agent, there were several exchanges of communication with Isabella Delgado. A Shalene, Texas. local described Ms. Delgado to me as being approximately sixty-five years old, about five feet four inches tall with a slender frame, and of Hispanic origin. Her now-deceased husband was Caucasian. Together, they had a twenty-one-year-old daughter. In addition, there was a thirty-two-year-old stepson from her late husband's previous marriage. After Delgado's husband passed, she asked that her surname be reverted back to Delgado.

The Shalene, Texas, local also mentioned that, when it came to property acquisition, Ms. Delgado relied heavily on the advice/ guidance received from her stepson. I was operating in accordance with directives from my first cousins. The first cousins had asked me to find a buyer for the family's 30.8 acres. The teleconferences evolved from a letter I sent to Ms. Delgado dated March 19, 2018, to a series of exchanges that can best be described as good old-fashioned haggling.

May 9, 2018:
Email from Joe Harris to Isabella Delgado

Me: Good afternoon Ms. Delgado. Just a note to confirm receipt of your April 23, 2018 offer to purchase the *heirs'* property in Shalene. I certainly apologize for the delay in my response. I have been addressing some rather pressing teaching and home repair concerns. In addition, a high priority for me is to keep my family members in the loop (for some it is the travel season). At this point in time, I cannot in all good conscience accept your offer of $400 an acre. The Shalene property has been in my family since 1898. Please consider offering a per acre amount that is closer to the fair market value of the property (Table 1, pg. 27). Someone mentioned that they believe you own a Chipotle Mexican Grill franchise in a neighboring city. If so, then it would have been great to talk to you in person about the Shalene property – Perhaps over a cup of coffee at your establishment. As noted in a previous conversation, I sometimes use Google Earth to view the Shalene property. It appears that at some point after 2005 you constructed a pond on your 90-acre site. I am very impressed by the project and probably would have asked you, over coffee, what techniques were used to make that happen. Once again, please consider offering a per-acre amount that is closer to the fair market value.

May 9, 2018:
Table 2 - Henderson County Appraisal District Sent to Ms. Delgado

Category (Vacant Land)		Values for Comparable Acres of Vacant Land	Per Acre Value
Assessed Value		$42,012 (30.8 acres)	$1,364.03
2016 Confirmed Sale		$103,425 (29.51-acres)	$3,504.74
2016 Confirmed Sale		$88,102 (30.38- acres)	$2,900
2016 Confirmed Sale		$72,300 (31- acres)	$2,332.26
2016 Confirmed Sale		$62,264 (31- acres)	$2,008.52
Average Value (confirmed sales)			$2,686.38
2018 Pittman's for 30.8 acres	According to:	Henderson Assessment District	$2,913.00
2018 I. Delgado for 158.0878 contiguous acres	According to:	Henderson Assessment District	From $2,138.00 (for 150-acres) to $1,915 (for 200-acres)
Suggested Asking Price:	For Pittman 30.8 acres	30.8 x $2,686.38 = $82,740.50	

Clue: This is an expanded version of the table that was presented to Ms. Delgado on April 19, 2018 (think backward)

Clue: A review of confirmed sales (including the assessment district notes) shows that the property should sell for $2,913.00 per acre (think backward)

May 26, 2018
Summary: Telephone Call from Breana Waraksa to Joe Harris

Ms. Waraksa indicated the following:

She preferred to talk via telephone as she was not "high tech" and did not have access to email.

She definitely wanted to purchase our property.

She received the second letter that I sent via regular mail to Annie Wyatt. (An initial letter was sent via certified mail and it was returned unopened.)

The thirty-six-year-old Waraksa is the daughter of the late Brenda Waraksa and granddaughter of the late Annie Wyatt. Annie Wyatt passed away about three months ago.

Breana Waraksa is now the sole family survivor.

Ms. Waraksa leases part of Annie Wyatt's land to Ms. Delgado (to be used for any purposes she wants).

She asked how much Ms. Delgado offered.

She scoffed at the $400 per acre value.

I mentioned the $1,300 per acre "baseline" value that appeared on the tax bill.

She would be willing to offer $600, $700, $800 (but not to the level of $1,000 per acre, etc.).

Adding that if she were to acquire our property, she viewed the "undivided interest" issues as a potential legal problem – that could translate into an expensive back-and-forth court battle with Ms. Delgado – involving multiple survey teams, etc. - For that reason, she was unwilling to offer a dollar amount that was at the level of $1,000 per acre, etc.

She said her grandfather built a pond on our 31 acres that was larger than the Google Earth, "blue tinted" pond that shows on Ms. Delgado's 90 acres.

She also said our 31 acres are on a hill (high ground) – with pear trees that bear jumbo-sized fruit –

In addition, there is an abandoned home up on that hill –

Also, when it rained, she said Ms. Wyatt's former 50 acres were on low ground and often got flooded from the runoff

She understood that Ms. Delgado really wanted our property – but was trying to "lowball" us.

She anticipated that there may be an undivided interest fistfight with Ms. Delgado over the dividing line between her 25 acres and our 31 acres –

Adding that she was not afraid of Ms. Delgado - In fact, Ms.

Delgado's lease with her was due to run out in a few months – and she planned to kick her out.

> **Clue:** Breana Waraksa would be willing to offer $600, $700, $800 - but not to the level of $1,000 per acre, etc. (Observe – but not just with the eye)

> **Clue**: Breana Waraksa viewed the "undivided interest" issues as a potential legal problem that could translate into an expensive back-and-forth court battle with Ms. Delgado involving multiple survey teams, etc. For that reason, she was unwilling to offer a dollar amount that was at the level of $1,000 per acre, etc. (Connect the dots. Connect Observation A to Observation B to Observation C, and so on)

May 27, 2018
Table 3 - Joe Harris Sent "Breana Waraksa Table" to Family

(The target amount was $1,791.35 per acre (including deductions for projected easement costs of $20,000 and survey costs of $9,000)

Category (Vacant Land)		Values for Comparable Acres of Vacant Land	Per Acre Value
Assessed Value		$42,012 (30.8 acres)	$1,364.03
2016 Confirmed Sale		$103,425 (29.51-acres)	$3,504.74
2016 Confirmed Sale		$88,102 (30.38-acres)	$2,900
2016 Confirmed Sale		$72,300 (31-acres)	$2,332.26
2016 Confirmed Sale		$62,264 (31-acres)	$2,008.52
Average Value (confirmed sales)			$2,686.38
2018 Pittman's for 30.8 acres	According to:	Henderson County Assessment District	$2,913.00
2018 Breana Waraksa for 197.41 acres (not known if it is contiguous): Brenda Waraksa 12.5 acres + Annie Wyatt 50 + acres = 62.5 + acres)	According to:	Henderson County Assessment District	From $2,705 (7.5 acres) to $2,039 (for 12.5 acres) to $1,936 (for all 197.41 acres) – e.g. the > the number of acres the < the per acre value. Ms. Waraksa owns 197.41-acres

Suggested Asking Price:	For Pittman 30.8 acres	30.8 x $2,686.38 = $82,740.50	
Legal Battle #1: Adjusted Asking Price: Survey Team (northern border)	For Pittman 30.8 acres	30.8 x $2,686.38 = $82,740.50 minus $9,000 (northern border survey team) = $73,740.50	$2,394.17
Legal Battle #2: Additional Adjusted Asking Price: Easement Rights Costs	For Pittman 30.8 acres	30.8 x $2,686.38 = $82,740.50 minus $9,000 (northern border survey team) = $73,740.50 minus $20,000 Projected Easement Rights Fight = $53,740.50	$1,791.35
Post Legal Battle #1: Adjusted Asking Price: Survey Team Costs + Road on the Southern Border (Ms. Delgado probably will not let us use her existing road)	For Pittman 30.8 acres	30.8 x $2,686.38 = $82,740.50 minus $9,000 (northern border survey team) = $73,740.50 minus $20,000 Projected Easement Rights Fight = $53,740.50 minus $9,000 (southern border survey team + access road) = $44,740.50	$1,452.61
Post Legal Battle #2: Adjusted Asking Price: Fencing Around the Entire Perimeter of the Property (unknown variable = type of fence)	For Pittman 30.8 acres	30.8 x $2,686.38 = $82,740.50 minus $9,000 (northern survey team) = $73,740.50 minus $20,000 Projected Easement Rights Fight = $53,740.50 minus $9,000 (southern border survey team + access road) = $44,740.50 minus $8,000 (unknown variable = type of fence) = $36,740.50	$1,192.87

May 29, 2018
Summary of Email from Houston, Texas–Based First Cousin to Joe Harris

According to my first cousin, she and her sister did not agree that I would pay $30,000, etc. to a lawyer and be reimbursed when and if the property sells.

Adding that they agreed that I would negotiate the best price I could get from anyone who wanted to buy the property. According to her, they were not interested in dealing with lawyers.

Clue: Obtaining a consensus vote among the first cousins sometimes proved to be problematic. For example, the first cousin noted above only held a 0.5 vote (her sister had the other 0.5 vote). However, she and her sister were not always on the same page when it came to various courses of action. (Identify patterns. What are recurring themes, things keep repeating themselves?)

May 29, 2018
Joe Harris Response to Houston, Texas–Based First Cousin

Good evening [name of first cousin], if legal fees emerged it was definitely my understanding that I had permission to pay those fees, and that I would be reimbursed for those expenditures once the property sold

The *Family View Summaries of Shalene Activities* (*FVSOSAs*) notes were structured to help clarify the latter issues as well as quite a few other issues

However now that you have clearly stated your position regarding legal fees etc. – it appears that Breana Waraksa's offer is the only logical way out.

A review of the *FVSOSAs* notes reveals quite a bit of information.... for example,

No one (other than the people who border us on the North, East, South, or West) will be willing to buy this property without an easement

We will need legal assistance to force an easement because Ms. Delgado has refused to voluntarily grant one

After an easement has been granted, we will have to pay a survey team to draw a clear boundary between Ms. Delgado's property and our property

After an easement has been granted, we will have to pay that same (or another) survey team to map out the route for a road – probably on the southern border

This is because Ms. Delgado will probably oppose a request to use her existing road that runs through the 5-acre strip on the South.

At some point we will have to pay a fencing crew to seal off and "gate" the property

Ms. Waraksa called on Saturday – and we had a preliminary conversation –

I have not called her back – because I needed to share the information provided by Ms. Waraksa with the family and obtain feedback/guidance from everyone who wishes to weigh in

I also needed to double-check some facts regarding Ms. Waraksa with the Henderson County Assessment District

Once again, if the family does not want to pool our money and fight for this property, then Ms. Waraksa appears to be the best option

It also appears that Ms. Delgado has elected to ignore my follow-up email request

In that request, I asked her to consider increasing the per acre amount of her original offer of $400 per acre to purchase.

Best Wishes,

May 29, 2018
Summary of Follow-Up Response from Houston, Texas–Based First Cousin

She thanked me for the summary/timeline of recent Shalene activity and indicated that It was very helpful.

She then reminded me that she and her sister were not interested in "lawyering up."

She then stated that very, very limited lawyer presence was requested.

Adding that she and her sister wanted to be free of the Shalene property and not to enrich the lawyers. Concluding, she stated, "We believe that you can negotiate."

> **Clue:** "We wanted to be free of the Shalene, Texas property, not enrich the lawyers. We believe that you can negotiate." (Identify patterns. What are recurring themes, things keep repeating themselves?)

May 29, 2018
Summary of Follow-Up From a Second Houston, Texas–Based First Cousin

She stated she was in agreement with the majority on the lawyer. She added, "If we really don't need one, why get one." She concluded by stating she would like to take a field trip there to see exactly what we will be fighting for.

> **Clue:** Similar to the sister + sister combo (where each had a 0.5 vote), this was a brother + sister combo (where each had a 0.5 vote). However, the brother and sister were not always on the same page when it came to various courses of action. (Identify patterns. What are recurring themes, things keep repeating themselves?)

May 29, 2018
Joe Harris Response to Comments from a Second Houston, Texas–Based First Cousin

Good evening [name of first cousin], thank you for the feedback.

It looks like I will be calling Ms. Waraksa soon – and try to do what I can to close the deal.

[name of first cousin] was referring to a lawyer – to help us fight for the property –

It does not appear that the family wants to fight for the property - so we don't need a lawyer to help us litigate

However, we still need a lawyer to look after the best interests of the family – in the "selling" process

I have had several conversations with Brett Hamilton, an attorney who is affiliated with the First Title Company of Shalene, Texas

Owing to his affiliation with the title company, Attorney Hamilton does not get involved with "litigation."

For at least the past month Attorney Hamilton's title company has been working on the title summary for our proposed sale

A titled summary will be required whether or not we

39

1. Sell the property (the family wants to go this route) or,
2. Go to court to try to force an easement (The family does not want to go this route)

Once again, what Attorney Hamilton can do is make sure that the selling process is conducted with the best interest of the family in mind

For example, we can ask him to include in the language of the selling agreement – the retention of the mineral rights concepts that you and I have discussed in the past

May 31, 2018
Joe Harris Follow-Up Response to Second Houston, Texas–Based First Cousin

Good evening [name of first cousin], thank you for your kind words of encouragement.

I believe in my last correspondence to the group I already indicated that we were not going down the litigation road.

I believe I also mentioned that the only logical avenue available to us was the granddaughter of the late Tommie Lee Wyatt.

A review of the "summary" documents I have sent to the group shows that I have spoken to quite a few Texas attorneys.

Several of them, especially the Shalene, Texas-based attorneys gave me some advice, however, they were not interested in taking on our proposed easement battle.

As you know, I received a surprise call from Ms. Waraksa Saturday night (Memorial Day weekend). Since the call came in the middle of the Golden State Warriors vs Houston Rockets playoff game – I turned the sound off – and turned my back to the widescreen. I think the "preliminary negotiation" conversation went very well – At the conclusion of the call, she understood that I needed to share her offer of $500 or $600 or $700 or $800/acre with the group.

I called [name of first cousin] the next day – and reminded her that a court battle - just for the easement rights - could cost as much as $20,000 –

A review of my summary notes shows that the $20,000 concept had already been shared with the family in a previous "summary" correspondence.

Judging by the surprise in her voice, it sounded like she was hearing the $20,000 figure for the first time.

At the time of my call [name of first cousin] was in the check-out aisle of a local retail store.

She said she would call me back after she got home and read the email about the $800 offer. I also asked her to call you as well as [name of her sister] – and ask you guys to read the email about the $500, $600, $700, $800 offer.

[name of first cousin] did not call me back that day – However, I received an email from her (I believe the next day) which indicated that her computer had been in the shop (she didn't mention that when she was in a local retail store)

I called the Henderson County Assessment District on Tuesday 5/29/18 – to get a better idea of the value of Ms. Waraksa's various properties – I was trying to obtain a better understanding of why she was offering such a low amount for our property. What I discovered was that Ms. Waraksa had inherited a lot of property.

So far I have only heard back from you and [name of first cousin], however (based on the feedback from you and [name of first cousin] I had enough "direction" to call her back on Wednesday, May 30, 2018 – In my last email to the group I informed you guys that I would do so,

Unfortunately, Ms. Waraksa is not very "high tech" – So she does not have an email, etc. All she has is the telephone number she gave me. I am not even sure of her mailing address

All I know is that I sent two letters to her late grandmother's house (one of them was Certified and returned to me unopened) –

Ms. Waraksa opened the second letter (sent by regular mail) - and called me in response to the letter.

So I left a message for her on Wednesday, May 23, 2018. She did not call me back

At the risk of not appearing too "eager" to sell at her $500, $600,

$700, $800 price – I left another message for her today. She did not call me back.

If I could have spoken with her, yesterday or today - my goal was to see if she was interested in a 5-year deal (similar to the purchase of a car) with a down payment + monthly payments, etc.

That is because she expressed some degree of financial concern – when it came to offering more than $500, $600, $700, or $800 an acre (She did not say $800 an acre – she cited the entire range)

I have attached the proposed deal to this correspondence.

If she was not in favor of the 5-year plan and - held firm to one of the values referenced in the telephone conversation (once again, she did not say $800 – she said $500, $600, $700, $800 – and that she definitely didn't want to pay $1,000 an acre).

Then I was going to settle on the best value available (hopefully it will be $800 an acre – maybe even $900 an acre)

I don't know whether or not she has a 40-hour-a-week job etc.

When she called Saturday night it was around 9:00 p.m. Central Time.

So tomorrow after around 6:00 p.m. or 7:00 p.m. Central Time – I will try to call her again

I don't know what's going on in Shalene, Texas with her - I can only hope for the best

I hope she is not having second thoughts about going up against Ms. Delgado (obviously Ms. Delgado wants the property for $400 an acre)

Ms. Delgado also knows she has us over a barrel – and since the *Heirs of Rosie* have decided they do not want to pool their money and fight her – she soon will realize that she has the power to force us to sell for $400 an acre

And $400 an acre is the exact value Attorney Cody James attempted to force the family to sell at four (4) years ago – when [name of first cousin] retained the attorney from Tyler Texas. Best Wishes,

May 31, 2018
Joe Harris Email to Family re: Updated Breana Waraksa Negotiation Table

Good evening all, I left a message for Ms. Waraksa on 5/30/18 – unfortunately, she did not call me back

I left another message for Ms. Waraksa today 5/31/18 – she did not call me back

I am unsure whether or not I will attempt to call her tomorrow 6/1/18 – Sometimes it's best to just wait a few days

She is "low tech" e.g. she does not have access to email

As you know, I currently do not have a cell phone – So even if she could receive a text message – I can't send her one

Once I talk to her – I plan to continue the discussion regarding a better price

However, if that does not go very well – I will see if I can get her to commit to an $800 or even a $900 per acre value.

June 1, 2018
Joe Harris Email to Family re: Updated Breana Waraksa Negotiation Table

Good afternoon all, so far Ms. Waraksa has not returned the messages I left on 5/30/18 and 5/31/18.

If/when she does return the call(s) I plan to present the attached revised schedule for her consideration

If we cannot reach agreement on the various assumptions that comprise the revised schedule

Then the default position will be the $500, $600, $700, or $800 per acre values she referenced in our one and only (so far) telephone conversation.

Since she is opposed to offering $1,000 per acre, hopefully, we will be able to agree on an $800 or even a $900 per acre value

I also plan to write her a letter and send it by regular mail to her late grandmother's address.

The letter will contain the revised amortization chart.

June 1, 2018
Joe Harris Email to Family re: Copy of Letter Sent to Breana Waraksa, June 1, 2018

Good evening all, so far no response from Ms. Waraksa to the messages I left on her system on 5/30/18 and 5/31/18.

Although I did not call her today, I have attached a copy of the letter that I sent this afternoon.

She should receive it by Monday, June 4, 2018

June 3, 2018
Joe Harris Email to Family re: Copy of Letter Sent to Breana Waraksa, June 1, 2018

Good afternoon all, I found Ms. Waraksa's Shalene, Texas address using an internet search engine.

The first letter was sent to her late grandmother's address.

If the mailman makes the right decision, Ms. Waraksa should receive the first letter on 6/4/18 (e.g., the mailman might decide to write "deceased" on the envelope and return the letter to me).

The second letter was sent to Ms. Waraksa's address on record (and takes the decision-making out of the hands of the mailman). Best Wishes,

June 6, 2018
Joe Harris Email to Family re: Copy of Letter Sent to Breana Waraksa, June 1, 2018

Good afternoon all, so far Ms. Waraksa has not called in response to the letter(s).

In the meantime, I have attached a revised "Amortization Chart" for your review.

I expanded the table to include the following down payment values; $4,000, $5,000, $6,000, $7,000, $8,000, $9,000, and $10,000.

Once we have identified a buyer, I anticipate that there will be title company fees (such as the title search fee of $1,500).

Therefore it would be ill-advised to suggest a down payment in an amount less than $4,000

Best Wishes,

June 9, 2018
Joe Harris Email to Family re: Copy of Letter Sent to Breana Waraksa, June 1, 2018

Good evening all, so far Ms. Waraksa has not called.
Earlier this afternoon I left a message for Edward Fontenette.
He owns the property just North of Isabella Delgado's 25 acres.
He did return my call and shared information regarding the deer hunting season
Best Wishes,

June 10, 2018
Joe Harris Telephone Call from Edward Fontenette (resides in Houston, Texas)

So far Breana Waraksa has not called to continue our "purchase" discussion
Mr. Fontenette called around 9:00 p.m. Central
Mr. Fontenette owns 32.9 acres North of Isabella Delgado's 25.2 acres. I first spoke with him on 4/2/18. I asked if he would reconsider purchasing the property. I offered him the same 4 – 6-year schedule that was presented to Breana Waraksa.

Mr. Fontenette indicated he was still in the process of clearing some of the brush on his 32.9 acres therefore was not interested in purchasing additional land at this time.

He drives to Shalene often from Houston, Texas – And although he did not know Breana Waraksa, he was familiar with the late Tommie

45

Lee Wyatt, the late Annie Wyatt, and Isabella Delgado. Since he was familiar with the area, he requested and was provided the addresses for Breana Waraksa as well as Annie Wyatt. He did not ask, and I did not provide him with Ms. Waraksa's telephone number

Regarding the deer hunting season, He indicated the following: (1) It usually starts around the first of October (for those with *bow & arrows),* (2) it starts in November (for those with guns). October is usually when the hunters put up the stands and the feeding stations (it is possible to leave these things out for the entire year). Deer hunting usually ends around the first or second week in January each year

June 18, 2018
Joe Harris Sent Email to Family, Subject: Follow-Up Letter Will Be Sent to Breanna Waraksa on June 18, 2018

Good evening all, so far no word from Ms. Waraksa. I plan to send the attached letter via certified mail tomorrow. The same letter will be sent via regular mail c/o the late Annie Wyatt.

Dear Ms. Waraksa,

I am writing as a follow-up to the two letters sent to you dated June 1, 2018, The first letter was addressed to you and sent c/o Annie Wyatt. Once again, thank you for your telephone contact on Saturday 5/26/18. As agreed I have shared with my family your interest in purchasing our 30.8-acre property in Shalene, Texas. The family has asked that I proceed with the process of arriving at a reasonable agreement on a purchase price. I tried calling you at [telephone number]. I left messages on 5/30/18 as well as on 5/31/18. So far, you have not had an opportunity to return the calls or respond to the letters.

A summary of information presented in my March 23, 2018 letter to your late grandmother, as well as information acquired since then is shown below;

- The parcel numbers for the family properties are: [insert four parcel numbers]
- On the Henderson County Platt Map (enclosed) the

combination of my family's 30.8 acres and Ms. Isabella Delgado's 25.2 acres shows 56 acres of undivided interest.

- According to the Platt Map my family's property is bordered as follows: (1) on the West by Annie Wyatt, (2) on the East by Isabella Delgado (90-acres), (3) on the North by Edward Fontenette, (4) on the South by Isabella Delgado (5-acres), and (5) on the South by an underground Texas oil or gas pipeline (probably inactive)
- The legal description for parcel number [insert parcel number] is shown below. [insert legal description]
- The 2018 assessed value for each of my family's parcels is $11,215. So, the total 2018 assessed value for the 30.8 acres is $44,860.
- According to the Henderson County Assessor's Office, 31 acres of similarly situated properties in the Sanchez School District (our property is located in the Sanchez School District) sold in 2016 for (1) $103,425 (29.51 acres), (2) $88,102 (30.38-acres), (3) $72,300 (31- acres), and (4) $62,264 (31-acres)

During our 5/26/18 teleconference, you expressed a willingness to pay a per acre amount that ranged from $500, $600, $700, and $800. I have provided for your consideration an alternative range of purchase options. The options reflect an average per-acre value. The average value was calculated using your highest offer ($800 per acre) and the Pittman family's 2018 assessed value ($1,456.49 per acre)

Please let me know if you are in agreement with any of the purchase options presented in the table. Also, please let me know if you require further clarification of any of the assumptions underlying the various options. However, if none of the options presented in the table adhere to your expectations, I remain open to any additional suggestions you might have. (In the interest of brevity the table was not included).

Sincerely,

June 20, 2018
Joe Harris Sent Email to Family, Subject: Lawyers Contacted
for Assistance with Shalene, Texas, Property

Good afternoon [name of first cousin)] I trust all is well with you and yours. Just a follow-up to your inquiry.... "By the way, are you working with any Lawyers?"

I have spoken with quite a few individuals throughout this process.

Regardless of whether I was talking to the assessment district, a Shalene-based real estate agent, the Sanchez School District, or the Shalene appraisal unit – the question they had for me was always the same

At what point will y'all consider retaining yourselves an attorney?

The only lawyer I have remained in contact with is Franklin Peters (lead attorney who practiced law near the Florida Panhandle).

Personally, out of all of the litigation-related attorneys I have spoken with, the latter attorney is the only one who has consistently demonstrated that he is worth his "salt."

I interacted with him closely in 2013 - At that time he was willing to assist us in the initial lawsuit against our family that was filed by Attorney Cody James.

However, I was informed by [name of first cousin] that you had retained an attorney and that he would handle the situation.

At that point, I discontinued my discussions with [name of lead attorney who practiced law near the Florida Panhandle].

Once a year the *Los Angeles Times* publishes a magazine titled "The Legal Best of the Best" I called each of the real estate attorneys listed in the magazine and was referred to Attorney Franklin Peters.

The latter attorney is licensed to practice real estate law in three states (including Texas).

The attorney has all of the current information and is monitoring our 2018 situation

His most recent recommendation to me was to obtain a "title summary" – Upon receipt of the summary he wants me to forward a copy to him.

A title summary will be necessary (1) when/if we are successful in locating a buyer, and/or (2) when/if we decide to take legal action to try to "force an easement."

The First Title Company of Shalene Texas has been working on the title summary for quite some time now

I need to give them a follow-up call – So far I have only asked for a dollar estimate for the cost of the summary –

However, a Shalene, Texas-based attorney informed me that the title summary will probably cost around $1,500.00

So far I have spoken with at least six (6) attorneys (listed below) regarding the Shalene, Texas situation.

Two do not litigate. One only takes the case after you have obtained an easement etc. One could take the case but said his retainer was $15,000 and the battle could end up costing as much as $20,000 – So in his opinion, it was not worth it for us to fight – e.g. we would be better off selling to a neighbor – but $400 per acre was too low

Although he has made himself available to provide advice and guidance so far Attorney Peters has not agreed to take our case

He did mention that he knew of a few Texas-based real estate attorneys he could refer me to should we decide to pursue legal action.

You may recall that a few years ago he was going to use a local Shalene, Texas-based attorney for the preliminary hearings – and fly in for the main hearing, etc.

You may also recall that a few years ago he had a strategy to buy back the lost 25 acres from Attorney Cody James for $400 an acre – but you guys were not in favor of that

In retrospect, we should have at least tried to purchase the 5-acre strip to the South of our property (the names of six attorneys contacted to date were provided in this correspondence) –

Best Wishes,

July 5, 2018:
Summary: Isabella Delgado Email Sent to Joe Harris

Isabella Delgado: Ms. Delgado indicated the following: (a) she would be willing to double her previous offer for the Harris family's

30.8 acres of undivided interest, and (b) the revised value of $800/ acre amounted to an all-cash offer of $24,640

Clue: The $800/acre value was still far below the $2,686.38 suggested asking price (always be a skeptic)

July 5, 2018:
Email Sent to Isabella Delgado by Joe Harris

Good afternoon Ms. Delgado, I trust you and your family had an enjoyable Fourth of July. Thank you for reaching out to me regarding the Shalene property. First of all, I want to say that I am not opposed to the offer you have presented. The next step will be to allow my two cousins in Houston, Texas another cousin in Cedar Park, Texas, and another cousin in Pasadena, California to weigh in. My two aunts as well as my uncle have passed – My remaining aunt is in a nursing home. My cousins have stepped up and, along with me, have been paying the taxes. Of course, I will also need to seek input from the family's legal advisor. I plan to contact my family first via email and then follow that up with individual telephone calls. I suspect many of them are taking advantage of this post-holiday period to travel and/or interact with grandchildren. Without sending out a single email and/ or making a single telephone call – I know this much

1. The family wishes to retain the mineral rights to the property that we have held since 1898
2. A title summary is now available to facilitate this process, and several family members have indicated they wish to visit the property and take pictures
3. Even if sold, the family members (myself included) just want to say goodbye to the land that our great-grandmother and grand-mother once walked

So, disregarding the 2018 average confirmed sales value of the property ($2,686.38 per acre) and the 2018 value assigned by the Henderson County Assessment District ($2,913.00 per acre) – There is still the matter of the 2018 assessed value of $1,456.49 – which appears on the annual tax bill

I would be remiss if I did not ask if you would be willing to agree to any of the 4-year, 5-year, or 6-year schedules on the attached file.

If so, then examples of possible sales amounts would include;

1. $4,000 down with monthly payments of $687.29 for four years,
2. $4,000 down with monthly payments of $559.48 for five years, or
3. $4,000 down with monthly payments of $474.36 for six years.

Once again, if none of the offers showing on the schedule meet your satisfaction, then I am not opposed to your original offer.

Once I receive your reply to this correspondence, I will continue to move forward with the process of bringing my family up to speed.

July 8, 2018:
Summary: Isabella Delgado Email to Joe Harris

Isabella Delgado: A summary of Ms. Delgado's response is as follows; (a) her cash offer included the mineral rights, (b) she had no interest in financing the property, and (c) an after-sale visit to the property would not be a problem

July 8, 2018:
Joe Harris Email to Isabella Delgado

Me: Good evening Ms. Delgado, thank you very much for the follow-up.

In addition to me, the relatives who have been paying the taxes include; (a) a cousin in Houston, Texas a cousin in Cedar Park, Texas (her sister), (b) another cousin in Houston, Texas, and (c) a cousin in Pasadena, California (her brother). I will give each of my cousins a call and provide you with feedback as soon as possible

July 9, 2018:
Joe Harris Telephone Message Left with the First Title Company of Shalene, Texas

Me: Prompted by my first cousins' steadfast instructions to sell, I left a message with the receptionist for First Title Company of Shalene, Texas: "Please ask Brett Hamilton to give me a call - The family has located a potential buyer. We would like his firm to draw up the sales agreement."

July 9, 2018:
Joe Harris Email to First Title Company of Shalene, Texas

Me: Good afternoon all, I am writing as a follow-up to the message left with your receptionist earlier today. The family has located a potential buyer for our Shalene property. In a prior teleconference, Brett Hamilton invited me to give him a call once I have located a buyer – and he would be glad to assist in the sales process. A family member asked me earlier today about Mr. Hamilton's fee for structuring the sales agreement. I do not know. The property is valued at over $82,000 however, the selling price will be $24,000 (cash). The family will be retaining 100% of the mineral rights

Last week your receptionist read me the following note;

1. the title summary has been completed,
2. it was on Mr. Hamilton's desk,
3. he was reviewing a few things,
4. I will be receiving a call from him shortly

I am certainly looking forward to talking with Mr. Hamilton regarding the proposed sale of the Shalene property

July 24, 2018:
Joe Harris Email to Brett Hamilton Regarding Investment Group Offer

I received the attached letter in the mail yesterday afternoon.

I notified my family immediately upon receipt.

If the Investment Group's offer holds for all four (4) parcels, then my family would prefer to sell to them

If the Investment Group turns out to be a valid offer then my family may or may not allow Ms. Delgado an opportunity to counteroffer.

August 28, 2018:
Summary: Joe Harris Received an Email from Investment Group Canceling the Offer

He appreciated all of the information and it was clear things were organized.

However, his co-investor has decided to pass, given there were too many unknowns regarding neighboring owners, lawsuits, etc.

That adds a level of risk he was not willing to take. When you combine that with the access issues, etc., this was just too problematic for his company to take on.

He will keep my property in mind, but as of now, they decided to pursue a parcel with better access and no prior legal issues.

October 5, 2018:
Joe Harris Called Isabella Delgado

According to Ms. Delgado, she called Brett Hamilton last week for a status update. Brett Hamilton informed her that he planned to send out the power of attorney documents for all the landowners. However, there could be delays linked to the undivided interest and locating all the heirs. He also indicated that he was in the process of untangling the web to ensure all the title information was complete. In addition, Mr. Hamilton planned to reach out to me to get the paperwork in order for the *heirs*.

October 5, 2018:
Summary: Isabella Delgado Forwarded Email to Joe Harris

Isabella Delgado: Ms. Delgado requested an update on the 30.8-acre purchase transaction from the Harris family and acknowledged that complications could arise because the proceedings constituted an undivided interest transaction.

October 6, 2018:
Summary: Isabella Delgado Forwarded Email to Joe Harris

Brett Hamilton: Mr. Hamilton indicated the following: he planned to revisit the transaction file that day, would contact Joe Harris, and the process would require affidavits of heirship that reached back several generations.

October 17, 2018:
Summary: Email from Brett Hamilton to Joe Harris

Brett Hamilton: A summary of Brett Hamilton's email to Joe Harris is as follows: (1) He asked the District Clerk's Office to retrieve an old file from storage; (2) he now had a better understanding of who the heirs of Rosa Edwards were; (3) he requested a certified copy of an affidavit of heirship found in the file, and planned to place the copy into the Official Public Records; (4) he may send his Attorney's Report, which broke things down in fractional shares; and (5) quite a few Affidavits of Heirship will be required.

October 17, 2018:
Summary: Email from Brett Hamilton's Assistant to Joe Harris

Assistant: A summary of the email sent to Joe Harris from Mr. Hamilton's assistant is as following: (1) the Title Commitment and the Examiners notes were attached, (2) also attached was the agency's form for the required heirship affidavit, (3) affidavit's will need to be filled out for every person listed on Schedule C by a non-family member, (4) upon receipt of the completed form, Mr. Hamilton will prepare the final copy and the parties will then need to sign and have it notarized, (5) document preparation for each affidavit of heirship is $250.00 and (6) they will all also need to be recorded at closing.

Clue: There was an affidavit of heirship already on file in the Henderson County Clerk's Office. Brett Hamilton obtained a certified copy of the affidavit and filed it in the official public records (think backwards)

Clue: Brett Hamilton's assistant provided key steps which needed to be addressed in the affidavit of heirship process. These steps included: (a) affidavits of heirship must be filled out for every person listed on Schedule C by a non-family member, (b) each completed affidavit needed to be signed and notarized, (c) document preparation for each affidavit of heirship was $250.00, and (d) the affidavits of heirship needed to be recorded at closing. Schedule C identified twenty-five family members. (Connect the dots. Connect observation A to observation B to observation C and so on)

Clue: I was concerned about the final dollar amount that would be divided up among the first cousins. For example, the Examiner Notes provided by the title company on October 17, 2018, listed twenty-five family members. When I multiplied 25 times $250, I obtained $6,250. Was the $6,250 value supposed to be subtracted from Ms. Delgado's $24,640 all-cash offer? If so, that would only leave $18,390 to be divided among the five (5) first cousins (always be a skeptic)

Upon receipt, I shared the details of the various offers made by Ms. Delgado with my first cousins. German poet and philosopher Friedrich Wilhelm Nietzsche (1844–1900) is often credited for penning the quote, "The devil is in the details" (*Der Teufel Steckt im Detail.*)

October 17, 2018:
Email from Joe Harris to Isabelle Delgado

I certainly do not wish to burden you with the nuts and bolts of the progress on my side of the equation –

However, it is important that I keep you posted on my forward progress.

In the past few days I have sent out 51 letters in an attempt to locate missing family members

Earlier today I received the following communication from [name of staff member from the First Title Co. of Shalene, Texas]

"Mr. Harris,

The Title Commitment and the Examiners notes are attached.

I have also attached our form for the heirship affidavit that is required.

Affidavit's will need to be filled out for every person listed on Schedule C by a non-family member.

Once we have the completed form back Brett will then prepare the final copy and the parties will then need to sign and have notarized

Please note: Document Preparation for each affidavit of heirship is $250.00 and they will all also need to be recorded at closing

Please let me know if you have any questions."

A total of 25 family members are listed on pages 1 and 2 of Schedule C.

There are a few names on the list that I wasn't even aware of (which means I need to send out additional letters

So the preliminary cost of this particular step will be $6,250.

The latter cost does not include attorney/notary and/or other legal fees for those assisting in the completion process.

Please discuss with your attorneys and/or financial advisors the feasibility of increasing your purchase offer

For example, in an earlier correspondence I mentioned that the value showing on the 2018 tax bill is $44,860

The latter value translates to $1,456.49 per acre (in contrast to the $800 per acre you have proposed

A summary of my reasons for requesting an increase is shown below.

The "Henderson County Appraisal District" values the property at $2,913 per acre

The average value of confirmed sales for Shalene property of similar size is $2,686.38 per acre

During our 10/5/18 teleconference I mentioned that all family members were not on the same page regarding the proposed sale

Increasing your offer will greatly assist the process of getting all family members to buy into the sale.

In our initial communication regarding the pending sale I mentioned that the property that has been in the family Since 1898

Clue: So the preliminary cost of this particular step will be $6,250.

The latter cost does not include attorney/notary and/or other legal fees for those assisting in the completion process.

Please discuss with your attorneys and/or financial advisors the feasibility of increasing your purchase offer

For example, in an earlier correspondence I mentioned that the value showing on the 2018 tax bill is $44,860

The latter value translates to $1,456.49 per acre (in contrast to the $800 per acre you have proposed (Notice the finer details, not just the glaringly obvious)

Clue: A summary of my reasons for requesting an increase is shown below.

The "Henderson County Appraisal District" values the property at $2,913 per acre

The average value of confirmed sales for Shalene property of similar size is $2,686.38 per acre

During our 10/5/18 teleconference I mentioned that all family members were not on the same page regarding the proposed sale. Increasing your offer will greatly assist the process of getting all family members to buy into the sale. (Notice the finer details, not just the glaringly obvious)

October 17, 2018:
Email from Joe Harris to Brett Hamilton

Me: Good afternoon [name of assistant], Thank you for providing the information regarding the proposed sale. I am seeking clarification regarding the following; It is possible that the buyer "may" increase her offer

Brett Hamilton: Ok.

Me: If, when that occurs can the "forms" be adjusted accordingly?

Brett Hamilton: All that will need to be done is to have everyone sign an Amendment to the Earnest Money Contract once it is drawn up unless he increases the offer before it is sent out for signature.

Me: The buyer has agreed to allow the family retention of 100% of the mineral rights

Brett Hamilton: Thanks for letting me know.

Me: Is that reflected in the language of the contract?

Brett Hamilton: When the Earnest Money Contract is drawn up, that will be set forth as an Addendum. Is the Seller retaining the right to use the surface for development (drilling/production) of the mineral estate they own?

Me: In addition to the $250 for each of the affidavits, will there be an additional deduction for a "title summary?"

Brett Hamilton: The title company charges an escrow fee and a premium for issuing an Owner's Policy of Title Insurance. The title premium is based on the purchase price. At $30,000, the premium would be $380.00. The Affidavits of Heirship come from my law office. They are not title charges. Until we know the number of sellers involved, it's not possible to estimate what it will take to put all this together.

Me: If so, what is the dollar amount of that additional cost? Will the family need to retain the services of parties (other than family members) to complete the affidavits?

Brett Hamilton: If I understand your question correctly, let's wait and see how much information the family can provide. We'll have a better handle on that then.

Me: Thomas Taylor is referenced on Schedule C – was he correctly listed as a family member?

Brett Hamilton: Yes. He is listed as an heir of Doretha Taylor in the Affidavit of Heirship in the District Clerk's file. Kindest regards, Brett

Clue: In addition to the $250 for each of the affidavits, will there be an additional deduction for a "title summary"? The title company charges an escrow fee and a premium for issuing an Owner's Policy of Title Insurance. The title premium is based on the purchase price. At $30,000, the premium would be $380.00. The Affidavits of Heirship come from his office. They are not title charges. Until we know the number of sellers involved, it's not possible to estimate what it will take to put all this together (Connect the dots. Connect observation A to observation B to observation C and so on)

I had hoped that as a member of the first cousin inner circle, I would be able to effect a change in their attitudes toward the future of the Shalene, Texas, property. However, the back and forth sell versus partition internal discussions between the first cousins continued. Unfortunately, the majority of my first cousins were still in favor of selling. However, due to the concerns that emerged from my interactions with Ms. Delgado, the first cousins encouraged me to explore additional potential buyers. Among other matters, the first cousins were concerned that property with a potential value in excess of $82,000 was being sold for $24,000. And so, I proceeded to identify and screen several new candidates. I identified these candidates from the query letters they sent after canvassing the Henderson county public records

The buyer we ultimately selected, Austin Cassidy, chose to structure the sale in the form of an options agreement. In accordance with the terms of the options agreement, the buyer would be allowed an unspecified amount of time to (1) structure the family tree, (2) file the affidavits of heirship identified by the First Title Company of Shalene, Texas, and (3) file various legal motions such as a suit to partition and a suit to obtain the easement rights.

In February 2019 (approximately two years prior to the issuance of the 2021 demand letter), I made a last-minute decision to accompany the prospective buyer during a property walk through. The intended buyer agreed that the first cousins had inherited a worst of the worst situation. We could not sell the property because we did not have the easement rights, clear title, and the property had not been partitioned. Because the land had been left to all the heirs of Rosie, several affidavits of heirship would be required. In sum, without the easement rights, clear title, and a partition, all the group of first cousins could do was pay the taxes.

November 14, 2018:
Summary of Email from Austin Cassidy to Joe Harris

Mr. Cassidy thanked Joe Harris for sending the background information and indicated that he and his wife were reviewing the information and would follow up the next day regarding a pathway forward

November 20, 2018:
Summary of Email from Austin Cassidy to Joe Harris

The email response began as follows: "As we previously discussed, my wife and I are very interested in purchasing your 7.7-acres in Henderson, Texas."

A summary of the Options Agreement presented by Mr. Cassidy is as follows:

1. the Options Agreement was necessary owing to the significant title and access issues that burdened the property
2. the Options Agreement would allow the couple time to attempt to clear the title and negotiate an access easement or explore other legal remedies that would provide access to the property.
3. the proposed Option Agreement was attached
4. Because I owned an undivided interest with several family members, he and his wife would need to purchase their interest in the property for the same price they were offering me.

If I and my family members agreed to enter into the Option Agreement, he proposed the following:

1. They would attempt to determine what title curative documents were needed to obtain clear/marketable title
2. They would attempt to obtain all title curative documents needed to obtain clear/marketable title;
3. If they were able to obtain what they believed was clear title to the property, they would then attempt to partition the property so that any owners of an undivided interest other than me and my family members would have their interest partitioned (separated from mine and my family's interest);
4. He and his wife would then attempt to negotiate with adjacent landowners to obtain an access easement to the property
5. If they were unable to negotiate an access easement to the property they would determine if it was cost effective to (1) explore other legal options; and if so, (2) initiate legal proceedings to attempt to obtain an access easement

If Mr. and Mrs. Cassidy were able to complete items 1-4 above, they would then exercise their option to purchase the property, meaning they would schedule a time with me and my family members so we could close on the property.

In addition to the above, Mr. and Mrs. Cassidy would

1. agree to pay for all costs they felt were necessary for them to obtain clear title and access to the property.
2. They would not ask me or my family members to pay for any of the expenses or reimburse them for any expenses incurred, regardless of whether they ended up completing the transaction with me and my family or not.
3. All expenses incurred would be paid by he and his wife, and not my family. The reason they would be agreeable to do this would be in exchange for me and my family allowing them

the agreed upon time in the option agreement to complete the work needed to clear title.

4. Owing to the possibility that he and his wife would incur substantial expenses should they enter into the proposed option agreement, they would require the following from me and my family members:

   a. All owners in the property will need to enter into the option agreement

   b. Everyone must agree to allow the option period to be extended indefinitely should they initiate legal proceedings to gain legal access to the property or partition the property.

   c. The reason for this being that this would be out of their control as to how fast they could complete the required tasks and they would be unwilling to initiate such proceedings if there was a chance that the option period would expire prior to them being able to complete the legal proceedings

According to Austin, all of the steps noted above were necessary as part of the process of establishing clear title. However, if at some point he determined that he was unable to complete all of the identified activities, the property would revert back to the first cousins. Conversely, if he was successful in addressing the terms of the agreement, the first cousins would be required to honor the up-front options agreement to sell all 30.8 acres for $33,880 (or $1,100/acre). My personal preference was that the family should not sell, and should retain the legacy of generational wealth. I also had several concerns regarding various clauses that were contained in the options agreement.

Clue: Austin Cassidy and his wife were both attorneys. However, they were not licensed to practice law in the State of Texas. They migrated to Texas from an eastern state in the United States. Their mastery of legal concepts was demonstrated in the structured options agreements. (observe – but not just with the eye)

Clue: I was concerned about the following clause; "Everyone must agree to allow the option period to be extended indefinitely should we initiate legal proceedings to gain legal access to the property or partition the property" (observe – but not just with the eye)

Clue: Although not as well versed in the legal field as the couple, it might be possible for me to complete some of the tasks outlined by Austin (observe – but not just with the eye)

Clue: If I was successful in addressing the latter tasks, the family would have the option to retain the legacy of generational wealth (eliminate the inessential)

Chapter Three

On the evening of February 8, 2019, I took a late-night flight from the Los Angeles International Airport (LAX) in California to the Dallas Fort Worth Airport in Texas. My goal was to join Austin Cassidy, the prospective buyer, on a walk-through of the property. Dallas was on Central Standard Time and therefore two hours ahead of Los Angeles (Pacific Time). Upon my arrival in Dallas, I couldn't help but notice the drop in temperature from 57 degrees Fahrenheit at LAX to 46 degrees Fahrenheit. I felt the full impact of the bone-chilling cold right down to a numbing sensation in the tips of my fingers.

Fortunately, I was able to retrieve my luggage from the airport carousel. The boots that would be needed for the trek through the Shalene woods were packed inside my luggage. However, the curbside skycap at LAX had warned me that owing to my late arrival, there was only a fifty-fifty chance the luggage would be there when I arrived in Dallas. After I picked up the luggage, I took an airport shuttle to the rental car site.

Most of the suspense-filled drive to Shalene seemed to occur in pitch darkness. The exceptions included sparse, overhanging highway lamps, and the occasional headlights from a fast-approaching vehicle in the rearview mirror. That vehicle turned out to be a major produce supplier delivery truck. Rather than allow the truck driver to continue to urge me to increase speed on an unfamiliar stretch of road, I signaled and moved to the right. There was one rather eerie moment when I drove over a rather large, dark body of water that was probably an area reservoir.

The veil of darkness interspaced with occasional overhead lighting made for a suspense-filled drive. The extensive stretch over a large body of glistening water prompted me to tighten my grip on the wheel. I was not familiar with all the bells and whistles of the rental car, so I didn't think to use the high beams, which would have provided 350 to 400 feet of visibility. As a result, I kept my eyes glued to the 200 feet of road made visible by the low beams.

Approximately one hour and 44 minutes later, I arrived in Shalene. According to my cell phone, it was 52 degrees Fahrenheit, still cold by my standards. Fortunately the rain showers had subsided. All that remained was sleet on the ground and in the trees. At first glance, the sleet resembled shards of scattered broken glass. The late-night arrival, lengthy drive, and settling in process meant I would get less than three hours sleep before the buyer's 8:00 a.m. scheduled arrival time.

"Mr. Harris?" asked a thin-framed, five foot, eleven inch young white man with dirty blond hair and dimples in his cheeks. Perhaps because I was the only Black male walking into the lobby.

"Yes, and you must be Austin," I replied with a smile.

"Great! So are you ready to go?" he asked.

"You bet!" I answered.

And with that brief exchange, we headed out to his car in the parking lot.

The first item on the agenda was to drive to Edward Fontenette's home. Mr. Fontenette was the owner of the 32.9-acre cow pasture just north of the family's property. Unlike me, Austin appeared to be quite comfortable programming and navigating the GPS coordinates using his cell phone. However, we did end up in an unmarked cemetery before he reprogrammed it.

"Well, Mr. Harris, maybe some of the ancestors requiring affidavits of heirship are buried here," Austin suggested.

"Perhaps so," I replied.

Mr. Fontenette, a six-foot-two inch, heavyset Creole with a receding hairline, was waiting outside of his Shalene home when we arrived. My first teleconference with him occurred on June 10, 2018. He called me in response to a letter I sent him asking if he would be interested in purchasing the property. Although he was not in the market to purchase additional property at the time, the teleconference marked the beginning of a great friendship. After exchanging a few brief comments, Mr. Fontenette climbed into his flatbed truck and commenced to lead the way. All along the route I kept fading in and out of listening to Austin's comments about his wife and growing young family, attempting to soak in every twist and turn and towering pine tree along the way. I found the natural beauty of the overhanging trees and rural terrain to be captivating, downright spellbinding.

A small herd of about fifteen bovine were waiting for us at the 32.9-acre spread just north of the Shalene property. They began to move toward us from all four corners of the fenced-in property. Each of the Holsteins appeared to be at least four feet ten inches tall at the shoulder. Research conducted after I returned to the Los Angeles area revealed the following about these two different breeds: Holsteins are the biggest cows of the dairy breeds and Jerseys are the smallest. It is possible for Holsteins to weigh more than 1,500 pounds. In contrast, Jerseys are around 1,200 pounds. In addition, Holstein cows are breed for meat and milk. From a physical perspective, Holsteins have the black and white, or sometimes red and white, coat pattern. The last time I was that up close and personal with large bovines was during my preteen summer visits to Mama Lilly's Farm in Hempstead, Texas. Mama Lilly was the mother of Uncle Jake, Julius C. Lilly.

In response to my saying "Looks like we got ourselves a welcoming committee!"

Mr. Fontenette replied, "The reason they are coming at us like this is they think they are about to get fed."

He turned to the truck bed and almost effortlessly hoisted a fifty-pound sack of feed onto his right shoulder. He then proceeded to dump the contents into the feeding trough.

At the conclusion of the feeding episode, Mr. Fontenette led the way across the pasture to a rear gate and down an uneven dirt road that contained embedded tire tracks. The first stop was a small-sized pond.

Mr. Fontenette commented, "I had a problem a while back with a beaver who got up in here and was clogging up the pond, but after a while, he went away."

Austin added, "Over there, I think I see signs where wild pigs have been foraging for roots."

Mr. Fontenette replied, "That's right, the good thing about hiking through here this time of year is that the snakes are in hibernation."

Larry Blackmon, a close friend of the family in Texas, once told me about the time a college football buddy invited him to go hunting. Although Larry didn't know much about hunting, he reluctantly agreed to tag along. After traveling a great distance, he found himself out in the middle of nowhere, surrounded by thick brush and heavy vegetation.

His six foot, one inch, stockily built football buddy instructed him to "stand over there next to that tree."

The buddy then handed Larry a rifle as well as a revolver that contained six shells. That was when the buddy turned, walked away, and soon disappeared into the brush. A short while later, about six to eight piglets came running out of the bushes, followed by the mama pig.

The mama pig commenced to charging at Larry like he had done something wrong to her. Larry fired one shot from the rifle and missed. He dropped the rifle and fired another shot from the pistol, once again missing the mark. As the mama pig continued to advance, he proceeded to empty out the revolver's chamber. However, owing to the rapid closing speed of the pig, the shots fell errant. That was when Larry threw the gun to the ground and clambered up into the adjacent tree. The mama pig proceeded to bang and claw up against the tree trunk, seriously intending to get at him.

A short while later, the buddy emerged from the brush with a deer slung over his broad shoulders. Observing the situation, he threw the deer to the ground. He then pulled a revolver from his waistband and fired one shot that hit the mama pig squarely between her eyes. Pulling a bowie knife from its sheath, he slit the pig's throat. At that point, Larry recalled thinking, *Now here I am out here in the middle of nowhere, alone with a* stone-cold killer!

My reflections shifted to Mr. Fontenette's comments about snakes. As previously noted, I was born and raised in Southern California. So my Houston, Texas, relatives would probably describe me as a *stone-cold city slicker*. However, I was no stranger to snakes.

In 1959, en route to Galena Park, Texas, when I was in seventh grade, I spent a week on Mama Lilly's Farm in Hempstead. There was no shortage of snakes on the farm. Although I didn't care much for the outhouse experience, I definitely looked forward to the meals. There was the daily breakfast menu of hot grits, eggs, bacon, and homemade biscuits served with maple syrup. Chickens wandered helter-skelter throughout the yard, so the kitchen table often resembled a fried chicken horn of plenty.

My brother Bob and I had been invited to stay with Uncle Jake and his family in Galena Park, which was a small, closely knit and predominantly Black middle-class community on the outskirts of Houston. Uncle Jake and Aunt Anne had two daughters, Connye and Judlyne, who were more than just my first cousins. To the contrary, I viewed them as adopted sisters. Without them, all the excitement and joy I experienced while interacting with new personalities and navigating a broad spectrum of preteen adventures would have been incomplete.

In addition to the brief stay on Mama Lilly's Farm, I also encountered snakes while exploring the heavily wooded area behind Uncle Jake's home in Galena Park. It wasn't unusual for reptiles to slither into the rather expansive, fenced in backyard. I recall early spring, when the blades of grass had grown one or two feet tall. One Saturday morning, Uncle Jake decided to tackle the overgrowth with his gasoline-powered lawn mower. There he was, dressed in sandals, shorts, and a white T-shirt, joyfully humming a favorite tune to the loud roar of the churning engine. Much to my delight, Connye and Judlyne screamed, "Ohh Daddy!" as the severed snake pieces and uprooted chunks of matted sod went airborne.

During my one-year stay in Texas I was enrolled in Fidelity Manor (FMH), a combined junior high and high school. In addition to being the FMH woodshop instructor and photographer, Uncle Jake also officiated the varsity football games. As a result, my brother and I sometimes rode the school bus to the Friday night skirmishes. Glancing around the bus, I couldn't help but notice the contrast between some of the jumbotron-sized players and the petite, yet smoking-hot cheerleaders. We sat, in front of the bus, right next to an open one-gallon container of heat balm. Upon entering or exiting the bus, the players used to dip a few fingers into the balm and smear it all over whatever ailed them. And because Fidelity Manor High was a combined junior and senior high school, we often attended the sometimes-raucous varsity basketball games on Friday nights. A particular basketball game played against a crosstown rival illustrated just how rowdy things could get.

As time wound down on the tied basketball game, a fight broke out in the wooden bleachers. Apparently, two staunch opponents had a difference of opinion regarding the pending outcome. My brother and I were seated close to where the scuffle originated. As the battle ensued, girls began to scream frantically. The astonished onlookers seemed to be equally divided between wanna-get-aways and lookie-loos. Some idiot thought it would be cool to pull the master power switch, plunging the entire gymnasium and its occupants into sudden darkness.

The unexpected blackout prompted some members of the audience to run out onto the hardwood floor. The accidental jostling of hyperexcited parties in the dark, in turn, led to sporadic outbreaks of additional skirmishes. Desperately seeking an escape from the chaos and observing the stampede of students rushing toward the main exit, I shouted, "C'mon, Bob. Let's go!" I selected a path that led us across the hardwood floor and toward the elevated stage area. We scrambled up onto the platform and took refuge behind the closed floor to ceiling stage curtains.

When the lights came back on, Uncle Jake was weaving his way through the crowd of totally freaked-out students. Apparently on faculty-appointed MP duty and armed with a baseball bat, he shouted, "Son! Son! Come here, son. I want to talk to you. Naw, naw, son! Don't you! Don't you run away from me!"

The quality time spent with Uncle Jake was priceless. As a paternal role model, he provided a new perspective to the single-parent household I had become accustomed to. I only wrote one letter to my mother during the Galena Park stay. In many ways, it highlights several unforgettable moments that occurred during my one year stay.

February 13, 1960:
Letter from Joe Harris (age 12) to Florence Harris (Mother)

How are you, we are fine. We have had snow for the past two days. The weatherman says it is the first time it has really snowed this way since 1958. It is Saturday, and the snow has started to melt now, but there are still traces of snow. I was lucky enough to take about 9 or 10 pictures before the snow started to melt. We have made two snow men and one is still half way standing but it is practically melted. I gathered up a couple of snowballs and ice cycles and put them in the freezer. There is a branch inside one of the ice cycles. Our basketball team was supposed to have played Baytown yesterday – Friday, but the game was called off because of the snow.

I hope you will have had a Happy Valentine's Day by the time this letter arrives in California. I forgot to put on one of the Christmas presents what it was. Well that thing shaped in a round circle is supposed to be a hot pot holder. I made it myself.

I am on the school track team. I am practicing to run the 100 yard low hurdles and the 440 relay. I might go out for some other things because our coach Mr. Eaton said we could go out for three track events and two field events or three field events and two track. But you must take at least two or more things. I have in my track equipment a pair of track pants and shirt, a pair of track shoes, and two baskets. I am supposed to have a pair of warm up shoes and a warm up shirt but they ran out of them. Uncle Jake has made Robert and I two dressers each one would reach the ceiling if it wasn't for about two inches.

There is a big pond in back of our house with baby fish in it. I guess the big ones are out in the deep part but the baby ones stay near shoreline and are easy to catch. I caught twelve baby fish and put them in a glass aquarium. I feed them goldfish food.

I have been taking quite a few pictures with my camera. The first roll didn't come out so good because Connye forgot to get the temperature of the water. There are some points that I have learned about developing film. I learned that when you first go into the dark room you set your clock and get your film out of the camera. Next you cut the light out. Then you put the film in with the developer and leave it in for about 3 minutes. Next you take it out and put it in the water, leave it in for about 5 minutes. Then you put it in the fixer – leave it in there for about 9 minutes and then put it into wash for about 30 minutes. While you're doing all this changing from one pan to the other you must be moving the film around and make sure all the film is in the pan. Then after you are through with it washing, you take it and hang it up to dry. That is as much as I remember. I have to learn the part about putting the pictures on paper.

Uncle jake says we are leaving Texas the best part of the year. Right when it's fishing and hunting season. Aunt Ann and their family make us feel right at home.

Say hello to everybody and give my regards to Aunt Maudelle and Celest

How are Ambitious and her cat friends getting along? Our Sunday School group has written off for some addresses of pen pals in that religion all over the world almost. I wrote a pen pal twice.

Did you hear about Jack Paar walking out on his show? I didn't get to see the show but I wish I had.

I will try and write more later. Good bye for now and have a nice week end. – Your Son Joe

p.s. Robert and I can really shoot our BB guns and Robert is doing better in his spelling. You are probably wondering what took this letter so long coming. Well I sent it a long time ago but I forgot to put the city and state I was sending it to. So they sent it back to me. I won't make the same mistake again. Will write again.

Note: Jack Harold Paar was an American talk show host, author, radio and television comedian, and film actor. He was the second host of *The Tonight Show* from 1957 to 1962.

> **Clue:** In retrospect, A potential hunting destination for Uncle Jake could have been approximately 200 miles to the north on the family's Shalene, Texas, property (think backward)

As our trio continued to walk up the inclining dirt road, we encountered a second, much larger pond. The group took turns taking photos and videos of the babbling pond. The rather large pond was actually situated on the heirs' property. By then the temperature had risen to 57 degrees Fahrenheit. Still cold enough to prompt an annoying trickle of mucus to ooze from my left nostril.

Austin proved to be a regular Inspector Gadget. Included among the items in his backpack were a GoPro camera, water, snacks and a machete. Although not as sharp as it should have been, the latter item would soon prove to be invaluable. The large pond was just the beginning of this fascinating sojourn through this legacy of generational wealth.

About halfway through a heavily wooded area, I began to speculate about flora, fauna and the potential water supply. From my research I learned:

- East Texas is considered to be the region east of Interstate 45 and west of the Louisiana border. The northern border of East Texas is Oklahoma. The southern edge of East Texas is the

Gulf of Mexico. East Texas consists of 38 counties, with a population of about 1.9 million residents.

- East Texas has a notable dogwood blooming season. However, it is also famous for its flowers. Among the most celebrated flowers in the region is the azalea.
- The Carolina Chickadees is a small songbird that is native to East Texas.
- Lake Shalene, one of the largest lakes in Texas, is located nearby. Lake Shalene not only offers an infinite supply of water but also hosts a variety of recreational activities.

In addition to the above, my research also unveiled the following facts about birds in East Texas

- Wood ducks reside near streams and lakes in North and East Texas. The nation's most common duck, the hued mallards, can also be found in North and East Texas
- The upper coast of Texas is definitely in a unique position to observe migration. Because the state of Texas is situated directly in the center of the Central Flyway, most birds that frequent this route travel through Texas and eventually through Upper Coast Texas.
- The avid bird watcher will be pleased to know that they can look for birds year-round in Texas. For example, great bird-watching opportunities are available during spring and hummingbird migrations, summer nesting, and fall hawk watches, as well as winter resident birds.

As we continued forward, I also began to wonder about the kaleidoscope of pastel-colored changes in foliage that were associated with seasonal transitions. In the springtime, did the magnolia bloom? Did hiking trails emerge that were lined by short, stout dogwood bushes and twenty-five- to forty-foot mature dogwood trees? I once learned in high school botany that the seasonal changes in foliage were due to a chlorophyll breakdown. For example, in the fall, owing to changes in the length of daylight and changes in temperature, the leaves cease their food-making process. As a result, the chlorophyll starts to break down, the green color disappears, and the yellow to orange colors become visible. The end result is that the leaves take on their red and gold fall splendor.

In addition to the above, the cooler fall nights and gradual narrowing of leaf veins prompts the majority of the sugars produced to be trapped in the leaves. And it is this abundance of sugar and light in the leaf that results in the production of vivid anthocyanin pigments that, depending on their pH, produce red, purple and crimson colors. Thanks to that high school botany class, I also learned that trees do not turn the same colors each fall. That is because of the variations in temperature, sunlight and moisture from year to year. As a result, individual trees of the same species that are growing together could show differences in leaf color owing to variation in the amount of sugar in the leaves and genetic predisposition.

Because the heirs' property was situated on high ground the bumpy road continued to take an upward incline. During a recent teleconference, the late Mr. Wyatt's granddaughter informed me of the importance of having property on high ground. Apparently, during the heavy rains, the water flows downward and floods the surrounding areas. As part of her inheritance, the late Mr. Wyatt's granddaughter now owns property that is situated in low ground areas.

Pointing to a barbed wire fence, Mr. Fontenette said, "I think right about here is where my property ends and your property begins, so it looks like we need to climb over that fence."

I was quite pleased that Mr. Fontenette used the phrase "your property" when addressing me. I was starting to get comfortable with the vision of this being "my family's property" and not just land that was soon to be sold.

However, I hadn't bargained on climbing over what I would later term the first barrier: a barbed wire fence. The way I saw it, I was out there in the middle of nowhere—and the process of straddling a barbed wire fence could end up poorly. So, it took a little bit of persuasion and an empty gasoline can Austin found for me to stand on. The general idea was to push down with my left hand on a non-barbed portion of the fence and combine the spring-action torque from the wire with an upward sling pf my right leg to get up and over. The heavy boots I was wearing simply gave me additional pause for concern.

Owing to the sinewy strength in his long legs, Mr. Fontenette didn't have any problems clearing the barrier. Surprisingly enough, I managed to get my five-foot eleven frame over the fence with no problems. Although not injured, a piece of Austin's jacket did come in contact with a barb. So, we successfully cleared this initial barrier, only to encounter thick brush and heavy vegetation. Similar to my observations the night before, there was sleet on the ground and in the trees. The sleet often resembled shards of scattered, broken glass.

We then walked down a long, winding dirt trail that was flanked by 100 foot tall pine trees. Austin, armed with that machete, led the way. Throughout the journey, my true preference was to gaze upward at the frosty beauty of the tree-lined horizon. However, the floor of the darkened woods was thick with ropelike vines. And if your foot hooked one of those vines the wrong way, you could easily be taken down.

As we carefully navigated our way through the dense brush and heavy vegetation, I couldn't help but think, *What if the vines wrapping around my boots from the floor of the woods were the symbolic hands of my ancestors grabbing at my ankles and imploring me not to sell?*

To my surprise, we encountered a small patch of yellow daffodils in an open clearing. It was as though the cluster of flowers were an early sign that spring would soon be on the way. Moving past the daffodils and about halfway through the passage, we encountered a second barrier: a six-foot-wide creek. The creek appeared to separate one side of the property from the other.

Austin attempted to persuade us to walk across fallen timber. However, owing to the instability as well as the moist, slippery surface of the fallen pine, that option was quickly ruled out. So, we decided to broad jump across the creek. It was at that point that I remembered I had packed so fast, I failed to include a second pair of pants. It just wouldn't do for me to board a return flight with my pants knees all muddy from the jump. I was a Los Angeles Rams fan, so I mused at the idea of buying an expensive pair of Dallas Cowboy sweatpants upon returning to the airport. Fortunately, I was able to grab the other side of the sloping ravine without brushing my knees.

As our journey continued, we discovered several large areas that could best be described as clearings. The open spaces were natural landing spots for a helicopter. Prior to the site visit, I had a teleconference with a local helicopter pilot. The strategy was that he would drop me off in one of the clearings and I would hike into the property and meet up with Mr. Fontenette. After the teleconference, Austin mentioned that he was opposed to the helicopter drop-off strategy as he was afraid of flying. The latter statement, in conjunction with the following voice mail message on my cell phone from the pilot, prompted me to scrap the helicopter option:

"Ah, Joe this is Will Robert from the Lone Star State Helicopter Service, I apologize for the delay, I have been having a few problems with my phone. However, I did send you an email with the prices and everything. I was kind of concerned about where you would land out there. I visited Google Earth and I am not seeing a really big area for a landing. I am seeing the pond and a bunch of trees. I will need a flat stretch, perhaps 100 foot by 100 foot minimum of clear grass. Perhaps I'll take another look at Google Earth. Anyways give me a call when you get a chance."

Addressing me, Austin said, "Mr. Harris, it's really easy to keep your bearings in here." That's when he showed me the Google Maps feature that was downloaded to his cell phone.

From my perspective, without Google Maps and/or a compass, the thick brush, heavy vegetation and meandering trails could have easily resulted in some degree of disorientation. When researching the question, "How many acres is a full-sized football field?" the resulting answer is about 1.32 acres. So, 30.8 acres (the heirs share of the former 56 acres) is almost 41 full-sized football fields.

It was at this stage of the journey that we observed deer hunting blinds as well as deer feeding stations positioned throughout the clearings. According to research I later conducted, blinds serve the purpose of visually hiding the hunter. Some blinds are designed to muffle sounds and reduce a hunter's scent to game. Of course hunters still need to be quiet in blinds and limit unnecessary movement so that they do not inadvertently alert the game to their presence. The white-tailed deer is the species native to the Henderson area.

Probably due to the rather chilly temperature, as well as the amount of hiking, climbing and jumping involved, I suspected Florence, my late mother, would have paused and waved goodbye to me at the barbed wire fence. For her, that probably would have been a déjà vu reminder of the time she watched me climb over that six-foot cinder block wall in pursuit of a burglar. Only this time she wouldn't be horrified by my actions.

Similar to her Houston, Texas–based brother Jim and sisters Maude, Anne and Geraldine, my mother sang in a choir. Choir rehearsals were held at Neighborhood Community Church in Los Angeles. The church was situated about a half block from our home on 48th Street.

For a brief moment, I closed my eyes and imagined her there with me in spirit for part of the journey. My mother was a firm believer in the power of prayer. So I am sure she would have enjoyed listening to traditional songs. On that day, however, I suspected contemporary music might have streamed from her earbuds.

Reflecting upon my mother's wide range of favorites, those songs probably included Harry Belafonte "Banana Boat (Day-O)," Sarah Vaughan "Gershwin Live! (with Los Angeles Philharmonic) Medley "But Not For Me," "Love Is Here To Stay," "Embraceable You," "Someone To Watch Over Me," Billy Eckstine "Fools Rush In (Where Angels Fear To Tread)," Nat King Cole "Unforgettable," The Platters "Only You," Nancy Wilson, "Face It Girl, It's Over," "Can't Take My Eyes Off You," Dionne Warwick "What the World Needs Now (Is Love)," Louis Armstrong, "What a Wonderful World," and as a flash back to 1959 (the year Bob and I were invited to stay in Galena Park) "Theme from a Summer Place," by Percy Faith and His Orchestra.

Addressing Mr. Fontenette, Austin said, "The inclining road we are taking seems to lead straight to the property."

"That's right," Mr. Fontenette answered.

Referencing the use of the private road to access the property, Austin added, "In Texas, a person has a right of access over a private road at all times and for all purposes."

That's when he asked, "Mr. Fontenette, would you be willing to grant me the easement rights to access the property?"

"Yes, I would," he answered.

Needless to say, my ears perked up when I listened to this dialogue. Lack of appropriate easement rights had been a major topic of discussion among the first cousins.

Austin then reminded us that he had agreed to referee his children's softball game and therefore needed to get me back to the hotel. Which was fine with me, because I had rescheduled my return flight so as to accommodate the 150-mile drive back to the rental car location.

We decided not return the same way we entered the property. I definitely approved of this decision because I wasn't looking forward to a rematch with the barbed wire fence. The alternate route allowed us to walk across one of the fallen 100-foot tall trees. The tree had conveniently come to rest on top of another stretch of barbed wire fencing. I would later refer to the second barbed wire fence as the third barrier. Needless to say, the fallen tree provided a welcome passage for my weary feet and legs.

A fourth and final barrier awaited when we returned to the cow pasture. Mr. Fontenette had locked the gate and was in the process of driving away from his property. That was when Austin put the car in reverse and attempted to back out of the muddy driveway that led from the road to the pasture. Unfortunately, owing to the recent rains, the tires had become entrenched in the muddy driveway.

Austin then placed the vehicle in idle and said, "Mr. Harris, I'll get out and push, and you put the car in reverse and apply the gas."

"OK," I replied.

I then exited the vehicle and took a few steps to the rear in an attempt to get Mr. Fontenette's attention as he was pulling away. He saw me waving him down, returned, and assisted Austin in pushing the car from the front, while I placed the car in reverse and applied the gas. The combined effort worked and the vehicle was dislodged from the rut, enabling me to back the car onto a dryer patch of road.

When I returned to the hotel, I took a few minutes to scrape and rinse the thick red clay from the soles of my boots. I then quickly gathered my belongings and checked out of the room. I still hadn't gotten the knack of it, so the desk clerk was kind enough to input the navigation features into my cell phone. And then I was off.

Of course the midafternoon traffic was a lot denser than the wide-open highway I'd traversed during the middle of the night. The two-hour drive back to the rental car location proved uneventful with the exception of an emergency stop. It appeared that the hike through the Shalene woods, including the scaling of the barbed wire fence, and broad jumping the creek had strained the muscles in my legs. So much so that sudden, involuntary contractions had developed in both legs. The muscle cramps forced me to pull over and stretch. Fortunately, the cramps subsided long enough for me to continue the trip back to the rental car office.

Unfortunately, the painful contractions returned during the two-and-a-half-hour-flight back to LAX. Fortunately, I was assigned an aisle seat. However, when seated, the leg cramps returned. In fact they were so painful that I chose to stand in the aisle, next to my seat, for most of the return flight. When the plane finally arrived at LAX, I was too proud to ask the flight attendant for one of the waiting wheelchairs. Instead, I chose to limp my way back down the long airport corridor and down the escalator to the baggage area.

That's when a tall brother who had the window seat in my row on the plane approached me from the rear and asked, "Are you going to be OK?"

I nodded yes in response to his concern. I then said, "I just hiked through my family's 30.8-acre property in Shalene, Texas. During the hike I climbed over a barbed wire fence and broad jumped a six-foot-wide creek."

The brother nodded that he understood. He then moved past me and continued forward toward the baggage area, glancing back long enough to say, "Now that will do it!"

For many. muscle spasms after exploring property would constitute a deterrent. For me, the severe cramps represented a red badge of courage and only served to further endear me to the land.

Chapter Four

Shortly after my return to the Los Angeles area, Austin sent approximately 100 photos as well as several videos of the Shalene excursion. I had a fairly new android and had not mastered the art of taking photos with it. However, I was able to take several videos of the property. Revisiting images of the terrain only served to reinforce my opinion that we should not sell. I called Austin and discussed the feasibility of backing out of the options agreement. He understood, and graciously agreed to allow the family to withdraw from the arrangement. Austin went a step further and provided the following useful clues for future actions.

Clue: The Pittman family/owners may need to file a quiet action title (estimated cost about $6,000). The latter step will provide clear title and avoid the need for approximately 30 affidavits of heirship. The quiet action title step may be necessary in the event that Ms. Delgado says no to the partition and no to an easement. If this happens, the Pittman family/owners may have to sue Ms. Delgado on behalf of the family (eliminate the inessential)

Clue: Definition: A quiet title action is a lawsuit that is brought in circuit court to clear a party's title to real property. The purpose of a quiet title action is to eliminate all claims to title, which might stand in the way of a title insurance company issuing a clear title insurance policy (connect the dots; connect observation A to observation B to observation C and so on)

Primarily due to the learning curve involved, it took several years to complete the majority of the tasks outlined by Austin in the options agreement. Tasks completed since 2018 have included:

- Used emails to keep the family up-to-date
- Interacted with several title companies on behalf of the family
- Retained the services of a private detective who performed cross checks by social security number and other tasks associated with verifying family linkages
- Structured the Harris Family Tree on ancestry.com
  - People 1,105; Records 1,759; Media 88
  - This step saved the family approximately $5,000 (the amount that a law firm staff member would have charged to complete the task)
  - The latter fee was quoted by a law firm in the North Texas Region.
- Structured and filed 28 affidavits of heirship
  - This step saved the family approximately $6,250

- The latter fee was quoted by the First Title Company of Shalene, Texas
- Structured and filed ten general warranty deeds,
- Discussed the easement rights pathway with Mr. Fontenette,
- Retained the services of a law firm in Southeast Texas, followed by a firm in the North Texas Region, and returned to the Southeast Texas law firm.
- Contracted with The Lone Star State Drone Company, who provided 1,450 images in 2D Ortho mosaic, and
- Established a Pittman Family Fund Account.
  - The voluntary proceeds were to be used for future activities associated with the Shalene, Texas, property

According to background research conducted when I returned to LA, snakes may not be the only problem in East Texas that is linked to tall grass. On July 28, 2023, the Center for Disease Control (CDC) issued the following warning: Alpha-gal syndrome: Meat allergy linked to tick bites rising. Apparently U.S. scientists have traced alpha-gal to saliva from the lone star tick. The allergy could trigger a life-threatening reaction to several types of meat or animal products. The lone star tick is identified by the white spot on its back. It is primarily found in southern and eastern parts of the U.S. However, experts warn that their range is expanding owing to climate change.

In addition to the above, Lyme-disease-carrying ticks continue to be an ever-growing concern. Lyme-disease carrying ticks can be found in all 48 contiguous states. As a result proper tick etiquette before and after any outdoor walk is important. In an article dated September 8, 2017, Dylan Stuntz, *American Forest* provided a summary of steps to take in addressing the Lyme-disease issue.

Although rare, typhus has been detected in warm parts of the U.S., including Southern California, Hawaii and Texas. Typhus is an infectious disease caused by bacteria that can spread from flea, lice and chiggers. Associated symptoms typically include fever, chills and body aches. In 2023 it was reported that a Texas man had his hands and toes amputated after contracting typhus from a flea bite.

A summary of findings from a 2023 Centers for Disease Control and Prevention report are shown below.

- Typhus is an infectious disease caused by bacteria that can spread from flea, lice and chiggers.
- Symptoms typically include fever, chills and body aches.
- Flea-borne typhus in particular usually causes nausea, cough, stomach pain and a rash from the bite that arises around day five of the illness, and
- Fleas and lice transmit the bacteria that causes typhus when the bugs defecate upon biting and the excrement infects the wound.

In addition to the above, on December 5, 2022 a news report addressed the topic; "Why a mosquito invasion is underway in Southeast Texas." The report cited high grass and puddles from recent rains as well as heat and humidity as contributing factors to the outbreak. According to my research mosquitoes should be considered dangerous to both people and pets. For example, the Asian Tiger mosquito and the Southern house mosquitoes are responsible for transmitting West Nile virus. Mosquitos have the potential to spread encephalitis and the Zika Virus. In addition, mosquitoes often infect dogs with canine heartworm. The canine heartworm is a parasite that, if not prevented against or treated, can be life-threatening. Mosquito prevention measures should take the following into consideration:

- Mosquitoes tend to swarm together near areas of standing water, especially at dusk and dawn (when they are most active).
- Mosquitoes hide and rest during the middle of the day, when temperatures are at their highest.
- Common hiding spots for mosquitoes include in tall grasses and areas of dense vegetation, along fence lines, in roadway ditches, along tree lines, and underneath decks or porches.
- Mosquitoes will enter inside homes in search of a blood meal.
- They enter through spaces found around windows, and doors, open windows and doors, or through tears found in screens.

- Prevention tips can be a great way to minimize exposure to mosquitoes
- However, the only sure way to render your property mosquito-free is with professional mosquito treatment services.

Initially during my March 2019 interactions with a Southeast Texas law firm I asked the lead attorney to investigate whether the Shalene, Texas property had been legally partitioned. The attorney, in turn, suggested that I have the land surveyed.

March 26, 2019

Dear Mr. Mitchell, (Shalene, Texas Survey Team Director)
Thank you for agreeing to provide cost estimates to survey my family's 30.8-acre property in Shalene, Texas. I understand that the earliest available appointment to conduct the proposed survey will be in two to three months. Owing to travel and work-related concerns, please schedule the survey for the earliest available Saturday. Also please let me know if, owing to a cancellation, a Saturday appointment becomes available prior to the two to three-month estimate.

The goals of the proposed survey will be to (1) draw a clear separation between my family's remaining 30.8 acres and Ms. Delgado's 25 acres and (2) identify the metes and bounds for an easement that will run through Mr. Edward Fontenette's 32.92- acre property.

The parcel numbers for the family properties are: [list four parcels for the 30.8 acres]

My family used to own [parcel number for 25.2 acres]. In 1986, the court awarded it to Tommy Lee Wyatt (deceased) who owned 50 acres to our west. Ms. Annie Wyatt (deceased) then decided to sell the 25.2 acres to Attorney Cody James. Ms. Isabelle Delgado purchased the 25.2 acres from Attorney Cody James in 2014. During the 2014 transaction Ms. Delgado also purchased a 5-acre strip to the South of our property (effectively locking us in on the North, East, and South). On the Henderson County Platt Map the combination of my family's 30.8 acres and Ms. Delgado's 25.2 acres shows as 56 acres of undivided interest.

According to the Platt Map my family's property is bordered as follows: (1) on the West by Annie Wyatt (deceased), (2) on the East by Isabella Delgado (90 acres), (3) on the North by Isabella Delgado (25.2 acres), (4) on the South by Isabella Delgado's (5 acres), and (5) on the South by an underground Texas oil or gas pipeline (probably inactive)

The legal description for [parcel number] is shown below.

[legal description]

The assessed value for each of my family's parcels is $10,504. So, the total assessed value for the 30.8 acres is $42,012. According to the Henderson County Assessor's Office, 31 acres of similarly situated properties in the Sanchez School District (our property is located in the Sanchez School District) sold in 2016 for (1) $103,425 (29.51 acres), (2) $88,102 (30.38 acres), (3) $72,300 (31 acres), and (4) $62,264 (31 acres),

March 31, 2019:
Summary: Email From Shalene, Texas, Survey Team Director

- He has reviewed the information that I provided.
- It appears that my family owns a total of 30.8 acres undivided interest in the defined 56 acre tract and Ms. Delgado owns the remaining 25.2-acres of undivided interest in the defined 56 acre tract.
- He is unable to establish where a division line separating the two properties would be without agreement by all parties involved.
- The latter step can be accomplished in two ways.
- One way is for all parties (all of the heirs of my family and Isabella Delgado) to come to an agreement as to how to divide the land which is commonly called a friendly partition.
- The second way is through the filing of a partition suit where the court divides the land because the parties could not come to an agreement.

- He recommended that I contact an attorney who is familiar with real estate law in Texas and discuss this with them.
- If all parties can come to an agreement and provide that information to him, he will then provide me with an estimated cost and time frame to perform the survey.
- His team does not work on Saturday.

Clue: "I cannot establish where a division line separating the two properties would be without agreement by all parties involved. This can be accomplished in two ways. One way is for all parties (all of the heirs of your family and Isabella Delgado) come to an agreement as to how to divide the land. That is what is commonly called a friendly partition" (think backwards)

Clue: "The second way that this could be accomplished is through the filing of a partition suit where the court divides the land because the parties could not come to an agreement. I would recommend that you contact an attorney who is familiar with real estate law in Texas and discuss this with him or her. If all parties can come to an agreement and provide that information to me I will then provide you with an estimated cost and time frame to perform the survey." (think backwards)

March 31, 2019:
I (Joe Harris) signed the first (of two) "Agreements for Legal Services" with the law firm based in Southeast Texas.

Scope of Services. Prepare partition demand letter.

Fees and Expenses. For the Firm to represent you, the Firm will require a non-refundable $1,450 retainer deposit to begin the legal services above.

April 1, 2019:
RE: 1986 Interlocutory judgment by the SE Texas law firm

John Peyton (First Lead Attorney) was in the process of trying to pull records from the 1986 [case number and district court]

- From what he could gather, Mr. Pittman et al. (the late James L. Pittman, Sr.) sued Mr. Wyatt (probably for trespass).
- Mr. Wyatt asserted a defense and claim of adverse possession yet before the trial on the cause was completed, the parties reached a settlement.
- The settlement included an agreement that Mr. Wyatt was conveyed interest in the property via deeds from the Remington's, Levi Jackson and the Kinkaid's.
- The settlement also included a finding that heirs of Rosie Edwards (Pittman and Jackson) are rightful owners along with heirs of Mr. Wyatt.
- However, the property was NOT partitioned.
- It appears that both Mr. Pittman et al. and Mr. Wyatt were both given undivided
- interests in the property.
- Attorney Daffin (legal counsel for the Pittmans during the 1986 Interlocutory Judgment hearings) states that she and the ad Litem attorney wanted the partition issue decided but the attorney for Mr. Wyatt did not agree.
- Further research will need to be done on Attorney Daffin' s subsequent efforts to partition the property.
- He will advise when he is able to get more information.

Clue: On April 1, 2019 the lead attorney from the Southeast Texas law firm confirmed the following; (1) the property was NOT partitioned, (2) It appeared that both James L. Pittman, Sr. et al. and Mr. Wyatt were both given undivided interests in the property, (3) the attorney for the Pittmans stated that she and the ad Litem attorney wanted the partition issue decided, but the attorney for Mr. Wyatt did not agree, and (4) further research will need to be done on the attorney for the Pittmans subsequent efforts to partition the property. (think backward)

As previously noted, it appears that during the 1986 Interlocutory judgment hearing, the elders accused Tommy Lee Wyatt (defendant) of trespassing. Mr. Wyatt asserted a defense and claim of adverse possession. The court denied Mr. Wyatt's claim of adverse possession, at which point he produced a deed that asserted that various parties, including someone named Levi Jackson, sold the property to him.

The Pittman attorney advised the family members to ask the judge to dismiss the jury and reach an out-of-court settlement. The elders then agreed to relinquish to Tommy Lee Wyatt 25.3 acres as part of an out of court settlement. The elders also asked for a partition of the 25.3 acres from the remaining 30.8 acres. However, for some reason the partition request was never implemented. As a result, Tommy Lee Wyatt had as much right to roam the 56 acres as the elders did. From that time forward, the property remained in an undivided state resulting in a tenants in common status.

June 4, 2019:
Summary of Teleconference Between the Lead Attorney from the Southeast Texas Firm and Joe Harris

- Lead Attorney - Recommended that he call Ms. Delgado, get her on the line and discuss the following concepts: (1) partition, and (2) implied easement of necessity
- Lead attorney - Sent an email follow up to Joe Harris: Apparently, Ms. Delgado referred him to her attorney
- If the teleconference with Ms. Delgado's attorney proved to be unproductive, a lawsuit could be filed against her.
- In reference to the lawsuit, she would be required to respond.
- According to the lead attorney, if I was concerned because both certified cease and desist letters were returned unopened (unable to forward, return to sender), for $75 the letter could be delivered to her by a process server.
- In reference to the cease and desist order, the lead attorney informed me that
- (1) nothing about the order was admissible in a court of law, and (2) no response was requested of Ms. Delgado
- The lead attorney also noted that "Even if Ms. Delgado received the order, she could simply ignore it and/or throw it in the trash can."

The latter comment was perplexing because the lead attorney had previously been in favor of the cease and desist route. Now he seemed to imply that it was not an effective way to go.

- The rationale presented by the lead attorney for the cease and desist order was to offset the possibility of Ms. Delgado claiming adverse possession, which was because it appeared that Ms. Delgado had been positioning herself to make an adverse possession claim.
- The lead attorney then recommended the "suit to partition" option first
- The latter lawsuit would also signal that we were willing to

go to court for the easement rights, the logic being, at that point, perhaps Ms. Delgado might be more willing to grant the easement.

Clue: So, the *revised* recommended strategy was:
   a. Suit to partition the property first – because it is a clearer kind of process (as opposed to an implied easement lawsuit, where we would have to petition the court to show a number of factors) and
   b. Then, as the suit progresses, we could add a non-compulsory joiner claim for an implied easement (think backward)

In reference to fees paid to date:

Lead Attorney: Joe Harris has an account balance of $1,100

Me: So, where did the $3,000 or so go?

Lead Attorney: Doc preparation, however if you are concerned about that – Ms. Delgado could still be served for $75.00

Me: At this point, I am requesting a discount on any proposed future litigation as a compromise for the approximately $3,000 that was already spent for the cease and desist order (which was never served)

Lead Attorney: There was some "labor" involved in the latter process – and if you wish I could have Ms. Delgado served (the cost for the service would be $75).

Me: I recommend that we move forward to the next step (a lawsuit) and that any discounts that can be applied (because Ms. Delgado never received the cease and desist order) would be greatly appreciated.

July 1, 2019
Summary: Email from the lead attorney for the SE Texas law firm to Joe Harris

- I spoke with Ms. Delgado's attorney, Bo Ryan "Bo" Maverick, who directed me to Brett Hamilton.
- When our firm originally took your case, we were unaware that you and Isabella Delgado had an undivided interest in a tract of land.
- Our understanding was Ms. Delgado was trespassing on your land from her adjacent parcel and allowing hunters to use your land. That was the basis for the cease & desist approach.
- Then we learned that you and Ms. Delgado each had an undivided interest in a tract of land.
- In that case to divide the land you will need to file a suit to partition.
- However, per Brett Hamilton the number of potential heirs is quite numerous.
- Therefore, we would not be able to move forward with a suit to partition until all affidavits of heirship are completed. Kind regards,

> **Clue**: I had several concerns with the content of the July 1, 2019, feedback received from the Southeast Texas lead attorney. At that point, the retainer was exhausted. I then proceeded to address the next steps on my own. Those steps included structuring the family tree, completing the affidavit of heirship process, and, out of an abundance of caution, retaining the services of another law firm based in the North Texas region (always be a skeptic)

November 17, 2020:
Letter from Joe Harris to Brett Hamilton

Dear Mr. Hamilton,

I have completed the process of structuring the affidavits of heirship for the family property in Shalene, Texas. I used the resources available on ancestry.com and Truth Finder.com to complete the forms. Yesterday I sent an ancestry.com email invitation to you to view the Harris Family Tree. I also used the attached *Heirs of Rosie* diagram as a guide.

As noted in my January 23, 2020 letter; the primary goal is to obtain clear title to the property. Once clear title has been granted, the family plans to partition the property by (1) asking Ms. Isabella Delgado for a friendly partition, or (2) filing a suit to partition against Ms. Delgado. Once a determination has been made regarding the partition, communications with a Shalene, Texas-based survey company will be resumed. The task of the survey company will be to (1) establish separation between [parcel number for 25.2-acres] and [parcel numbers for 30.8 acres]. The survey company will also determine the metes and bounds for the *easement* rights to the family's 30.8 acres. Once these steps have been completed, the family will decide whether it wishes to retain or sell the property.

The *Heirs of Rosie* used to own [parcel number for 25.2-acres]. In 1986, the court awarded it to Tommy Lee Wyatt who owned 50-acres to the west. Ms. Isabella Delgado purchased the 25.2-acres from Attorney Cody James in 2014. During the 2014 transaction Ms. Delgado also purchased a 5-acre strip to the South of the family property (effectively locking the 30.8 acres in on the North, East, and South). On the Henderson Platt Map the combination of the family's 30.8 acres and Ms. Delgado's 25.2-acres shows as 56 acres of undivided interest.

I provided a legal description of the property in a letter dated January 23, 2020. In the letter I also shared the similar property sales values that were provided by the Henderson Assessor's Office. I plan to re-contact the Assessor's Office to obtain more up to date sales values.

The Examiner's Notes (attached) identify twenty-five family members. However only twenty-four family members were deceased at the time. Margaret Price was not deceased. Contact information for Margaret Price can be provided upon request. Since the "notes" were made available to me, Geraldine Pittman Wooten has passed away.

Also, the following family members were not included in the Examiner's notes; John Barnes, Laral Barnes, Percy Lee Barnes, and Robert Taylor Murphy. However, affidavits of heirship have been completed for the latter parties.

Completed affidavits of heirship for the following family members were sent as attachments to the January 23, 2020 letter; (1) Maudell P. Williams, (2) Foster M. Pittman, (3) Howard B. Pittman, (4) Ann P. Lilly, (5) Robert M. Pittman, (6) Florence P. Harris, (7) James L. Pittman and (8) Walter A. Pittman. Since then, an additional twenty-three affidavits have been completed, and will be signed and notarized shortly. Your response to the following questions would be greatly appreciated:

1. Since Margaret Price is not deceased, will an affidavit of heirship still be required? If so, then I have attempted to complete an affidavit for her.
2. Should affidavits for the following deceased family members, not identified in the Examiner's Notes, be filed with the county clerk? John Barnes, Laral Barnes, Percy Lee Barnes, and Robert Taylor Murphy
3. Hector Dave Pittman DOB October 19, 1915; DOD October 19, 1915 and Rosena Pittman DOB January 1, 1917; DOD December 13, 1917) both died as children. Will affidavits of heirship be required for Hector and Rosena? If so, then I have already completed affidavits for both of them.
4. What dollar amount will be due payable to your firm for the "Clear Title Report?" I believe you mentioned the fee would be $1,500.

In order to complete the affidavit of heirship process, I retyped (in Microsoft Word) the affidavit of heirship PDF file that you sent to me. The clerk in the Henderson Courthouse informed me that a re-typed form in Microsoft Word would be acceptable.

The clerk in the Henderson Courthouse also informed me of the filing fee for the proposed affidavits. "The fee will be $26 for the 1st page and $4 for every 3 or 4 pages (per document) thereafter – there will be no charge for any extra name to be indexed."

Over the past few years I have either (a) initiated discussions with or (b) retained the services of various attorneys regarding this process. I understand that the family may, once again, have to retain the services of legal counsel to complete the future steps outlined in this correspondence. Sincerely,

> **Clue**: The letter formally advised Brett Hamilton that the sale of the Shalene property to Isabella Delgado was no longer on the table (Disengage from the task)

> **Clue**: Brett Hamilton did not reply to the November 17, 2020 letter. In fact the last communication from Brett Hamilton occurred on October 17, 2018 (Always be a skeptic)

December 1, 2020:
Summary: Teleconference with Attorney John Allen

Attorney John Allen practiced law in a city that straddled the regional divide between South and Central Texas. I was referred to him by a neighbor in the Los Angeles area. The neighbor was the owner and founder of a Southern California–based escrow company.

The Texas-based attorney recommended the following:

- I should locate a Texas attorney in a Northeast Texas city who specializes in real estate law as Shalene, Texas, is geographically remote
- The proposed attorney should file a motion for discovery that will include all records and bank accounts
- I should include trespassing, "waste" (e.g. Ms. Delgado messed up the property during use)
- The proposed attorney should request that Ms. Delgado not destroy any files, records, etc.
- This is because she (Ms. Delgado) should have offered to share the proceeds from the deer hunting operation

- In sum, he recommended a three-pronged attack
- I should ask all relatives to contribute to the fight
- He estimated that the fight could cost as much as $25,000
- He estimated the retainer for the partition and easement rights will be $25,000
- He then recommended that I sell the property to regain expenditures
- My relatives should be approached to share in the legal costs
- He indicated that I am following all the correct steps to secure the property – e.g. file affidavits of heirship, obtain clear title, request a friendly partition
- Take Ms. Delgado to court if she refuses to grant the friendly partition
- Follow up with Mr. Fontenette for the easement rights
- Otherwise, there will be another court battle with Ms. Delgado for access via the 5 acre strip that borders the county road
- He reminded me that people have a right in Texas to easement egress, etc.
- In his opinion, Ms. Delgado was being somewhat disingenuous when she offered $400/acre, and then $800/acre, while allegedly leasing out the land for $5,000 a year without the family's permission
- I should find people who knew my family for the signatures on the affidavits of heirship
- For example, it's not like they will have to appear before Judge Judy
- People will have up to three years to appeal the accuracy of the affidavits of heirship
- All that is necessary is that they knew the family – not so much that they knew every single detail about the deceased family members –
- See if there are any church folks who knew the family
- For example, the president of the Shalene, Texas, branch of the NAACP
- He recommended that I pay Mr. Fontenette money to have his deed amended for the easement rights

Clue: The attorney recommends a three pronged attack; (1) file a motion for discovery that will include all records, and bank accounts, (2) include trespassing, "waste, (3) request that Ms. Delgado not destroy any files, records etc. - This is because she should have offered to share the proceeds from the deer hunting operation (connect the dots)

Clue: The attorney indicated that I am following all the correct steps to secure the property, e.g. file affidavits of heirship, obtain clear title, request a friendly partition (think backward)

Clue: The attorney recommended that I take Ms. Delgado to court if she refused to grant the friendly partition and follow up with Mr. Fontenette for the easement rights. Otherwise there will be another court battle with Ms. Delgado for access via the 5 acre strip that borders the county road. I should pay Mr. Fontenette money to have his deed amended for the easement rights (always be a skeptic)

April 23, 2021:
Joe Harris Letter to Owner of a Law Firm Based in North Texas

I am seeking an attorney who is licensed to practice real estate law in Texas and who specializes in *easement* rights. Please let me know if a member of your firm is available to assist my family in achieving full title to property located in Shalene, Texas. My family has owned 30.8 acres of property in Shalene, Texas since 1898. The parcel numbers for the family properties are: [parcel numbers for the 30.8 acres]. My goal is to (1) complete the process of obtaining clear title, (2) obtain either (a) a friendly partition or (b) a court ordered suit to partition from a neighbor, and (3) retain a survey team to map out the metes and bounds of (a) the partition and (b) the *easement* rights path. On 3/29/21 a total of 28 signed, notarized affidavits of heirship were filed with the Anderson County Clerk's Office. In addition, I have structured the Harris Family Tree on ancestry.com.

Since 10/17/18 I have been following "clear title" as opposed to "quiet title" instructions from Brett Hamilton [telephone number]. He is either the owner of, or has agency rights to a Shalene, Texas company (First Title Company of Shalene, Texas). On October 17, 2018 [name of staff member] (First Title Company of Shalene, Texas) sent the following resources; (1) Examiner's notes, (2) Title Commitment, and (3) the title company's form for the required heirship affidavits.

April 28, 2021:

I paid the law firm based in the North Texas Region $2,000 for consultation services

May 4, 2021
Joe Harris Teleconference Attorney Danny Wilks - First Attorney, Law Firm Based In North Texas

First Attorney: What is the family's end goal?

Me: To obtain, clear title along with the easement rights after that retain the property for 1 or 2 years, visit the property, take pictures, have a picnic and/or reunion on the property, and then decide the next step

First Attorney: Do you want to sell the property?

Me: Not at this time. The property has been in the family since 1898 (123 years). Is it possible to overturn the 1986 Interlocutory Judgment? Will you first seek a friendly partition and then a court ordered separation?

First Attorney: The courts tend to avoid overturning "old Judgments" e.g. old judgments tend to not get "un-done" – It is a kind of "stability policy."
The family should have challenged the 1986 judgment back in

1986. I think a suit for partition is the route to take. The peer land can be divided. So,

Option #1: divide the property

Option #2: sell the property and divide the proceeds

(the latter option is not necessary because of the size of the property (e.g. 32-acres) – You will need to determine everybody who owns the property For example, there are a bunch of people on your side of the equation,

So the "set-up" will be: Person A + their interests, Person B + their interests, Person C + their interests.

A survey will have to be conducted to determine the metes and bounds - "here's where we want the lines to be drawn" - "However, be careful! Because the property is not accessible" - "Because of 'access' the value of the property will vary – depending on where you are." The surveyor will have to put some creative energy into the process of drawing the lines"

Easement versus partition - These are two (2) separate things

The goal should be to determine the most economical way to address the concepts of easement and partition

Questions to consider: Did the heirs landlock themselves?

What is the easiest way to access the property? What is the most straightforward way to proceed from (a) a legal perspective?, (b) a cost perspective?

Therefore, the neighbor to the North – who is willing to grant the easement – might be the most straightforward (cheapest) way to go – as opposed to a back and forth with Ms. Delgado over the 5-acres strip to the South route

The focus should be on not spending a lot of money fighting in court – when there is another way to access

However, if accessing the property via Mr. Fontenette's cow pasture doesn't work, then yes – fight Ms. Delgado for the route over the 5-acre strip

By all means, you should consider all of your options

Me: Should we ask Ms. Delgado for her financial records (e.g. proceeds from the deer hunting operation?

First Attorney: As 'tenants in common" Ms. Delgado has a right to the use of the property. Which could include excluding the Harris family. The question is "would we (the Harris family) have done the same thing, if we were in Ms. Delgado's position?"

There will be a 'timing' issue – e.g. how far back did the deer hunting operation go?

Another issue is - How much money are you willing to spend fighting over the deer hunting property lease – when compared to how much you expects to receive?

A summary of your priorities:
Priority #1: Clear title – who are the owners?
Priority #2: Easement
Priority #3: Partition
Priority #4: Fighting over the deer hunting leases

A summary of your goals
Goal #1 Easement right
Goal #2 partition

With respect to the above, if Isabella Delgado says no to the friendly partition – then a lawsuit will be filed e.g. a partition lawsuit to divide her out

Goal #3 (e.g. deer hunting operation) might not be worth the cost

Title commitment – I should send that to him again. He will follow up with the First Title Company of Shalene, Texas – ask them to look through + update it – then say "OK"

Selling price - Is there a price the family would consider?

What would you consider selling for? Keep in mind that the biggest determinant to value is easement and the need to be partitioned

Getting other family members on board - This process may or may not be "a hassle"

Henderson County Appraisal District Values - Property value could increase a few years down the road

The family needs to move forward on the partition - Ms. Delgado is probably not going to agree on how the properties should be partitioned and she is probably going to want to extract every penny out of the deal

Survey Team - You really need to get in there with a survey team so that you can see what you are getting yourself into.

First Attorney: The original marching orders from the North Texas-based law firm was to conduct discussions with the family, make sure everybody was on the same page, and use the general warranty deed and or waiver process to reduce the number of owners. The goal was to render the pending suit-to-partition more manageable. For example, if 20 individuals owned the property, then 20 subpoenas would have to be served. The charge for each service would be approximately $150. The fees for the pending lawsuit could become quite insurmountable. Therefore, the attorney stated that he might be in favor of a more cost effective mediation approach.

Clue: A summary of your priorities:
        Priority #1: Clear title – who are the owners?
        Priority #2: Easement
        Priority #3: Partition
        Priority #4: Fighting over the deer hunting leases (connect the dots)

September 3, 2021
Summary: Joe Harris Teleconference with the First Attorney
From the Law Firm Based In North Texas

- He has attempted to contact Ms. Delgado, but so far, no response. He thinks trying to negotiate out of this situation would be a good idea, thereby avoiding the need to litigate. He can see the value of it at this stage; there is no reason to go to court if we can resolve it without litigation, especially if Ms. Delgado shows a desire to work it out
- Yes, the waiver forms I submitted to the First Attorney will suffice –

- The next step will be a conversation with Ms. Delgado to see if this matter can be resolved on better grounds – Get some kind of agreement in play – get everybody on board
- Then a survey will be conducted (Ms. Delgado will be present). The goal should be to conduct a single survey (there should be no need for Ms. Delgado to conduct a second survey) – That way both sides will save money
- So get everybody on the same page – If the matter went to litigation – the judge would probably order that the case go to mediation
- So it is possible that we can work out some kind of deal anyway – Mediation does make sense – as it comes without the expense of litigation – Maybe we will end up going to mediation outside of litigation. However, there is still value in the proposed approach – e.g. resolve the matter without litigation
- They (Ms. Delgado's team) will see that you (Joe Harris) are locked in e.g. you have already consolidated your interest – therefore what is needed is a good offer to get this done –
- So it is OK for you (Joe Harris) to send him (the First Attorney) an email with all the "contact" information – If we get everybody on the same page – then the mediation process should be a little easier – Since you (Joe Harris) have already consolidated on your side – they (Ms. Delgado's team) should see that you are going to protect your families' interest

I provided the following summary to the First Attorney;

- The process of structuring the general warranty deeds, beginning with Geraldine Pittman Wooten (Aunt Geri). Aunt Geri experienced difficulty paying the annual property taxes on her 7.7-acres. I stepped up once and paid her back taxes. The second time I was asked to pay her past due taxes, I asked for a formal transfer of the 7.7-acres to me. Aunt Geri graciously complied.
- I also had an opportunity to reach out and get to know members of other family lines. The property was left to all the Heirs of Rosie Edwards (my great-grandmother).

- Rosie had eight children: Mattie, Green, Lou, George, Bessie, Elma, Rebecca, and Cora. Elma Edwards gave birth to my mother, Florence Harris, and therefore was my grandmother.
- My sister Rowena, brother Bob, and Jabari, the son of my late sister Lynette also transferred their interest to me. As a result, the encumbrance report structured by a national title company determined that I owned Aunt Geri's 7.7 acre parcel as well as Aunt Maude's 7.7 acre parcel.
- In addition to Aunt Geri's transfer of interest, I also received transfers of interest from the descendants of Bessie Edwards, as well as the descendants of Cora Simmons Edwards.

Clue: The First Attorney: provided the following summary of the priorities:
> Priority #1: Clear title – who are the owners?
> Priority #2: Easement
> Priority #3 Partition
> Priority #4: Fighting over the deer hunting leases (connect the dots)

Clue: The First Attorney: I should consider buying out "others" interest to keep the process manageable (Eliminate the inessential)

Clue: The First Attorney: Regarding "adverse possession," Ms. Delgado is a tenant in common who is locking us out. The latter fact "weakens" her adverse possession claim. She can still attempt to claim adverse possession – however the courts will probably not rule in her favor. It is not as easy to claim adverse possession, when Person A - in a tenant in common situation - adversely claims adverse possession over Person B – So, adverse possession will not work for Ms. Delgado (Notice the finer details, not just the glaringly obvious).

> **Clue: The First Attorney:** Regarding easement rights – He recommended that I work something out with Mr. Fontenette – because it is the easier "easement" route - I have a much better relationship with Mr. Fontenette than with Ms. Delgado – So,
>
> Contract A – men get along with each other (this is a generic expression)
>
> Contract B – persons don't get along e.g. the slightest little thing and one of the parties will attempt to sue the other (Identify patterns. What are recurring themes, things keep repeating themselves?)

September 27, 2021
Surprise follow up call from Attorney Julius Johnston - Second Attorney who also worked for the North Texas Region law firm

After providing substantive information during the September 3, 2021 teleconference, the assigned First Attorney for the firm based in the North Texas Region unexpectedly departed the agency. Apparently the Second Attorney had been tasked with clearing the first attorney's workload. In contrast to the First Attorney, the Second did not seem to share the First Attorney's optimism in regard to the four priorities.

Second Attorney: For a number of reasons, including decisions made by my deceased relatives – It appeared to him that the only option available to my family – was to sell to one of the two neighbors that had us boxed in. This was the only way to try to recover some of the money we have put into it.

Second Attorney: You can seek contribution or reimbursement for expenses off the top – however all parties (owners) must agree. For example; The target sales amount could be $20,990.51 (amount paid so far by Connye, Darilyn, Joe and Wally).

Ms. Delgado once offered $24,620 So, $3,649.49 would be distributed in direct proportion to fractional ownership.

In reference to the $1,500 I unsuccessfully attempted to pay the First Title Company of Shalene, Texas for clear title, the second attorney stated; First Title Company of Shalene, Texas did not accept the payment, because their receipt of funds was dependent on the closed sale of the property to Ms. Delgado.

Me: I am willing to pay $10,000 to your firm for a suit to partition.

Second Attorney: I don't like to see my clients spend an excessive amount of money and not achieve the kind of outcome they are expecting. In other words, the partition will not get a result you want. Adding, even if you were able to get Ms. Delgado out, your problems with her are not going to go away. (Unfortunately the Second Attorney did not elaborate).

I encourage you to step away from any emotional attachment to the property. In a court of law emotional components count for nothing. For example, argument like we have had the property since 1898 and Ms. Delgado just acquired her property in 1996 and 2014 respectively. Or your family doesn't like her because of the aggressive manner in which she has attempted to gain control of all of the property.

In addition, I am not in favor of the equitable" distribution of acres chart that you have structured (the chart on page 112 was based on dollars spent). Dollars spent is not the appropriate way to determine ownership. So, you will get only what you are entitled to. You can't partition the property based upon dollars spent.

Adding, you are mixing two concepts that don't go together. There is no way to divide the property. The only way is to sell.

"when did Isabella Delgado acquire the 25-acres and the 5-acre strip?"

Me:"In 2014"

Second Attorney: "was there ever a time when the family had the *easement* rights – and were not boxed in?"

Me: "initially the family had the easement rights, however Henderson County allowed new owners to purchase parcels that boxed us in."

Second Attorney: From the second attorney's perspective the only thing that mattered was the "title report" And the title report – displays, among other things, "ownership"

So all the things that you (Joe Harris) have done – were "very beneficial" in his eyes. That includes structuring the family tree on ancestry.com, structuring and filing the affidavits of heirship, and structuring and filing the general warranty deeds.

Because the affidavits will help determine who owns what

So, according to the second attorney, my task will be to obtain an "updated" title report that reflects the newly "recorded" affidavits of heirship and general warranty deeds

Adding, for example, that I might find that I own $1/11^{th}$ of 1/3 of 55%

Which could amount to a one acre sliver cut out

So, according to the second attorney, the general warranty deeds are linked to the concept of "transfer of interest" And transfer of interest is linked to "ownership."

The second attorney also underscored the fact that - the property is showing in the books as 56 acres of undivided interest. That means Ms. Delgado (the encroaching neighbor) – is a major "owner" – because she now owns 25 of the 56 acres.

So, according to the second attorney, it looks like my last "financial" acts on behalf of my family will be to (1) order the title search report, and (2) Pay the attorney to oversee and possibly mediate the paper work – of any proposed sale - noting that his reimbursement rate is $300/hour

He asked who was [name of first cousin])? (Apparently he had an opportunity to view the family email exchanges)

He then asked "who was the person in the photos?"

As it turned out, that was a rear image of me – when I visited the property in 2019. I also mentioned that if you enlarged the image – you would see the "green" deer hunting station in the background

Once the teleconference ended, I recalled thinking, Hopefully I will be able to "smooth the waters and get back online with Ms. Delgado or the late Tommy Lee Wyatt's granddaughter. I also recalled that Ms. Delgado had once mentioned that she would not be opposed to the family visiting the property every now and then, even if we no longer owned it.

Clue: The following statement explains why it was eventually determined that Walter A. Pittman, Jr. was not an owner. It was true that his father, Walter A. Pittman, Sr., was a sibling to the elders, Maude, Anne, and Jim. However, he was not a participant in the elders four-way ownership distribution process.

"In addition, I am not in favor of the equitable" distribution of acres chart that you have structured (the chart on page 101 was based on dollars spent). Dollars spent is not the appropriate way to determine ownership. So, you will get only what you are entitled to. You can't partition the property based upon dollars spent.

Adding, you are mixing two concepts that don't go together. There is no way to divide the property. The only way is to sell." (connect the dots)

Clue: "I don't like to see my clients spend an excessive amount of money and not achieve the kind of outcome they are expecting. In other words, the partition will not get a result you want. Adding, even if you were able to get Ms. Delgado out, your problems with her are not going to go away." (observe but not just with the eye).

The latter statement did give me cause for concern. However, since the Second Attorney did not elaborate on "your problems with her are not going to go away," I was unclear as to a possible interpretation. The Second Attorney strongly encouraged me to sell to Ms. Delgado. A table which illustrates various aspects of the proposed sale is shown below. However, because my true goal was to retain the property, I elected to double back to the previous firm based in Southeast Texas.

September 8, 2021
Table 4 - Distribution of Proceeds From the Sale of 56-Acre Shaline, Texas Property If Sold for the 2020 Average Price of $185,000

Owner	Payment for Ownership/ Taxes Paid/ Misc.	Balance > Isabella Delgado Payment	Acres Owned	% of Total	To Be Paid by % Ownership > Isabella Delgado Payment	Total Amount To Be Paid Escrow Fees + Taxes Not Included
I.D.	$83,250	$101,750	25.2	0.45	N/A	$83,250
J.H.	$13,360.84 Taxes + Shaline, Texas	$88,389.16	19.95	0.35625	$28,107.57	$41,468.41
Cousin 1	$300 Shaline, Texas related	$88,089.16	3.62	0.06464	$5,099.99	$5,399.99
Cousin 2	$4,938.95 taxes	$83,150.21	3.62	0.06464	$5,099.99	$10,038.94
Cousin 3	$4,251.78 taxes	$78,898.43	1.81	0.03232	$2,549.997	$6,801.78
Cousin 4	0.00 Co-owner with Cousin 4	N/A	1.81	0.03232	$2,549.997	$2,549.997 So, cousins 3 + 4 = $9,351.774

Among other parting instructions, the second attorney from the law firm based in North Texas strongly recommended that I obtain an "updated" title report that reflects the newly "recorded" affidavits of heirship and general warranty deeds. I later learned that the report he was referencing was termed an encumbrance report. In general, a property ownership and encumbrance report contains:

- Current vesting
- Full legal description
- Current tax information
- Open mortgages
- Open liens secured by the property
- Unsecured liens and judgements pertaining to the owner
- Title chain and related documents
- Current and prior owner liens and judgments

A summary of my efforts to obtain the encumbrance report is shown in chronological order below.

September 28, 2021
Summary Telephone Call To Second Title Company of Shalene, Texas

- A staff member indicated he was experiencing a family emergency – so his ETA would be a little delayed – he referenced a run title on acreage only (on sub division) on a run title
- He cautioned that if I ordered it from them I could end up paying $500 + tax and then paying the same fee again once I had a buyer (closing costs)
- He referenced a $250 starting fee for legal description, ownership and encumbrances reports
- He suggested I call the First Title Company of Shalene, Texas, and ask them if they could do it from the last document to include new updates – reference to title sheet, run sheet – where title sheet – run sheet

September 29, 2021
Summary of Telephone Call to the First Title Company of Shalene, Texas

- A staff member stated he would need a full legal description of the property along with the email
- He indicated that they were *running about 45–60 days behind* due to volume

- He stated that I could get an "encumbrance report" but not a title report for about $250
- He informed me that in order to get a title report I will need a "contract" – e.g. the property is in the process of being sold to someone
- He stated that the proposed encumbrance report would not take into consideration all those affidavits of heirship, etc.
- He informed me that the proposed encumbrance report would just show who the owners were and if there were any liens on the property

September 29, 2021
Summary of Follow Up Call to the Second Title Co. Made in an Effort to Avoid the 45–60-Day Delay

- The staff member asked me to send him an email that specified exactly what I wanted. He also indicated that there was a distinction between a new title report and an encumbrance report
- He stated that a new title report would be generated only if I had a contract to sell, e.g. a buyer in mind
- He added that, if all I wanted was an update on the title, an encumbrance report was the way to go
- He indicated that an encumbrance report would show limited ownership. The cost would be a little more than $250 and the researcher would run the title, review new docs – affidavits of heirship, general warranty deeds,
- He requested that I include a full legal description of the property and state that I was looking for "vesting"

October 5, 2021
Summary of Joe Harris Teleconference with Attorney Keith Jones - Second Lead attorney from Southeast, Texas law firm;

Second Lead Attorney:
What is your goal? To keep it or sell it?
Not permitting access (narrative fact)

Ms. Delgado has denied my family the easement

Ms. Delgado may have already achieved Step #1 in a *claim ouster* - e.g. in an effort to state "I am claiming full ownership"

You have already done the heavy lifting

You should alert the County Appraisal District regarding taxes

"We are not trying to pick a fight with Ms. Delgado.

The "Firm" definitely can help

He is willing to make a phone call – in an effort to avoid litigation

Docs to be sent to him: (1) 1986 Interlocutory Judgment, (2) Proof of filing of the affidavits of heirship + the general warranty deeds

Allow him to view the Harris Family Tree

Send him the existing title report as well as the examiner's notes

You should again consider offering to buy out my *first cousins*, thereby purchasing their interest

In lieu of the above, the property can be divided in accordance with your preliminary "ownership" calculations of 19.70762, 3.38226, 3.38226, and 3.38226

October 8, 2021
Summary of Joe Haris Teleconference with the Second Lead attorney from Southeast Texas law firm;

Second Lead Attorney:

The "Firm" needed me to sign an agreement for legal services

Actions could include: A demand letter for partition or cordially reaching out to Ms. Delgado's attorney – in an attempt to kick this thing off

As this moves forward, family members may elect to sell or transfer their interest to me

In answer to my question regarding majority versus minority "collectively, with 30.8 acres - Joe + Connye + Darilyn + Wally (family member at large) are already the majority owners"

Once again, as the process moves forward, things might change – as Connye or Darilyn may elect to transfer their interest to you

This will only increase my size – The goal should be to keep it in the family

Yes, he received the docs I sent on October 5, 2021

Yes you (Joe Harris) did the math correctly – in terms of the "even" re-distribution of un-allocated interest to all four owners

You have already ordered an "encumbrance report"

The report will reflect the updated "vesting's" from the recently filed affidavits of heirship and general warranty deeds

Joe Harris indicated he is still in the process of polling his family

OK I look forward to hearing from you next week

October 9, 2021
Summary of Joe Harris Email to Selected Family Members

Good evening all, "Together we stand, divided we fall."

A Houston, Texas-based law firm has agreed to continue the mediation process and, if necessary, to file the suit to partition

Still awaiting your input regarding Option 1, Option 2, or Option 3

October 11, 2021
Summary of Response of Family Members to an October 9, 2021 Email Sent by Joe Harris

So Where Do We Go From Here?

I have listed some options below – along with their pro and con features – I am certainly open to any other options group members may wish to share

Option #1

Continue forward with the suit to partition with the four "owners"

After successfully winning the suit, divide the property into four (4) parts in direct proportion to "ownership."

Pro

The family retains the property

I plan to construct a fence to keep Ms. Delgado etc. out

However, I do not plan to construct a fence to partition my area off from the family

All family members will be able to roam throughout my area – Unless someone does harm to the landscape (e.g. litter + trash, defacing the trees etc.)

Con

The annual tax bills will be adjusted to reflect appropriate ownership – So, there will be a substantial increase in my share of the annual tax bill. In addition to the $10,000, $11,000 or $12,000 fee for the suit to partition - I will be primarily responsible for the projected Mandatory Costs – and this could result in a "money pit" scenario for me.

Of course all, family members will be encouraged (but not forced) to contribute to the Pittman Fund – to help defray some of these costs. Remaining owners will be encouraged (but not forced) to share in the projected mandatory costs – in direct proportion to their percent ownership

1. M - fee for the survey team – Includes identifying each owner's parcel
   a. $3,500 (This is an average value – It is possible the survey could cost less)
2. M – fencing which separates family's 30.8 acres from Ms. Delgado's 25-acres
   a. $1,715 (estimated value, therefore could be more, could be less)
3. M – law firm fee to amend Mr. Lyles' Deed for the easement rights
   a. $2,000 (The dollar value for the easement strip still needs to be negotiated)
4. M – prefabricated pedestrian bridge over a 7-foot-wide stream
   a. $2,778 (Cost of the preferred bridge – there are lesser priced bridges)

Grand total for Projected Mandatory Estimates = $9,993.00

Option #2

Buy out Connye and Darilyn at the land locked rate of $400 an acre.

Owing to the pending lawsuit fees + projected mandatory costs, I am (Joe Harris) financially unable to offer more"

Pro

I will be able to stand toe to toe with Ms. Delgado in terms of percentage ownership within the 56 acres of undivided interest

The property will remain with the family – and "access" will be made available to all family members

This will help reduce the possibility that someone might elect to default on their taxes (which has occurred in the past)

Or threaten to break from the group and sell their share to someone cold canvassing the Anderson County records (which has occurred in the past)

Con

I was hoping Wally (family member at large) and/or his family would be able to participate in the buy-out

However that may not be the case at this point in time.

Option #3

Sell to Ms. Isabella Delgado

Pro

All "owners" should be able to regain some or most of their money

Con

The property will no longer belong to the family

The Initial Responses to Options 1 – 3 From Family Members/owners (shown below)

First Family Member "My family truly believes you need to be reimbursed for your expenditures" – so I vote for Option #3

Second Family Member "Joe, My vote is for Option 3-Sell the property. Sell all 30.8-acres to Ms. Delgado"

Third Family Member "Option #3 - Hi All, Sell the property…But I would love to kick Ms. Delgado off the property"

Fourth Family Member "I'm up for Option #1 – Continue forward with the suit to partition with the four "owners"
After successfully winning the suit, divide the property into four (4) parts in direct proportion to "ownership." **BUT I THINK FAMILY MEMBERS WOULD AGREE THAT WE DON'T NECESSARILY NEED TO DIVIDE THE PROPERTY INTO FOUR PARTS. That is unless that's REQUIRED???**

Fifth Family Member "Option #2 Buy-out Connye and Darilyn at the land locked rate of $400 an acre. Owing to the pending lawsuit fees + projected mandatory costs, I am financially unable to offer more" (Joe Harris)

October 18, 2021
Joe Harris Email to Second Lead Attorney S.E. Texas Firm

Good afternoon Attorney Jones. Thank you very much for your patience in this matter
The family has agreed to go forward with the suit to partition – as long as I pay all the legal fees.
So far, I have already paid over $11,000 on behalf of the Shalene, Texas property

The latter value includes approximately $2,794 paid to the Southeast Texas firm

Of course the pending encumbrance report will add another $250 + to the tab

The family's goal is to retain the property –

If maintenance and upkeep prove to be too costly – we will revisit this goal

The only way I can regain dollars spent – off the top - is via a joint agreement among owners – upon completion of a sale

I understand that your goal is to conduct mediation first. I will call and make sure I understand the possible ramification of the mediation first approach on overall costs.

For example, one of my goals is to ensure that mediation does not result in a significant increase in expenditures

Hopefully, a one hour mediation, at $385 (your hourly rate) will suffice

Preliminary topics for the proposed one hour mediation might be (1) a friendly partition, and (2) easement rights across the 5-acre strip to the south

Of course the friendly neighbor to the North is still willing to allow access via the outer edge of his 32.9-acres cow pasture

I am not opposed to having two (2) access routes to the property

The goal is to avoid an on-going mediation that does not succeed and only adds $2,000 etc. to the invoice

The $2,000 etc. plus an additional $10,000 (previously quoted by the Southeast Texas Firm) could have an adverse impact on me

It wasn't easy getting my family – and especially the four owners on the same page. Connye Yvette Lilly Turner and Judlyne A. Lilly are sisters – and elected to "share" ownership

The remaining owners are Joseph Harris, Darilyn Pittman Thomas and Walter Pittman Jr. (member at large)

I am definitely ready to continue the process of securing property that has been in the family for the past 125 years.

It is Ok to give me a call, or I will call you – Best Wishes,

The directions received from the Southeast Texas law firm included:

1. Obtain encumbrance (ownership) reports for each of the *first cousins* and
2. Coordinate with the *first cousins* to decide between a suit to partition (my preference) and a suit to sell all 56 acres (the *first cousins'* preference). From the very start, the Second Lead Attorney for the Southeast, Texas law firm has been understanding, encouraging and supportive of my Shalene, Texas-related efforts. His personal position was that 56 acres was quite a bit of land, and there was no reason to force the sale of all of it. This is particularly true given the fact that the property had been in the family since 1898.

October 19, 2021
Summary of Joe Harris Teleconference with Attorney Keith Jones - Second Lead Attorney

Second Lead Attorney:
   He could serve as your attorney (negotiator) or as the mediator
   The goal is to get them to come to the table
   We should at least approach the other side and present our idea to resolve this matter
   Your family could agree to sell to you (which is the outcome he prefers)
   Normally the Southeast Texas firm is hired to draft a demand letter
   If you (Joe Harris) can work out a deal with the firm
   Then they can turn their attention to Ms. Delgado
   In general, the firm is hired to draft a demand letter
   Or we can sue Ms. Delgado for the partition
   Of course, a demand letter could be viewed as a rather contentious approach and thereby is a rough way to kick it off
   However, we need to have some teeth behind our words

He will consult another law partner to determine the best approach to get this off the ground

Because, if we tip our hand, Ms. Delgado's people may "rush" to file a suit to partition against us – and that would have an adverse impact on us

So there is some "risk" involved here in terms of what information we could hold back

The "invoice" will be all at once, e.g. not one invoice for a single telephone call, followed by another for the suit to partition – In other words, there will be only one "invoice" and not a "double" invoice

So, a demand letter to Ms. Delgado will state

Either you agree to enter into a partition or we will sue if you have not complied within "x" number of days

He will call me tomorrow morning – He is aware of the time zone differences

Q: When was the last time you spoke to Ms. Delgado ?

Me: I have not spoken with her in about two years – There were law firms involved, first the Southeast Texas firm then the Law firm based in North Texas, and now the Southeast Texas firm – and *I know better than to speak directly to her when I have legal representation*

On October 21, 2021 I signed the second of two "Agreements for Legal Services" with the Southeast Texas law firm. I then discussed with the lead attorney the feasibility of comparing Levi Jackson's signature on the 1986 deed to his signature on his draft card as well as his driver's license.

October 21, 2021
Joe Harris Email to Keith Jones - Second Lead Attorney, SE Texas Firm

I am more inclined to go with the "partition letter" (fee = $1,450) as opposed to the telephone "reach out" (fee = $385)

My last email (correspondence) with Ms. Delgado was about July 5, 2018

From that time forward she (Ms. Delgado) has just continued to keep doing what she is doing

Since that time, the family actually considered selling to three other potential buyers

I reviewed the notes from Attorney John Peyton (First Lead Attorney, SE Texas Firm - your former law associate) – he reached the same stage that you are approaching – e.g. He actually reached out to

Bo Ryan "Bo" Maverick (Ms. Delgado's attorney) as well as Brett Hamilton (Shalene First Title Co.)

After his conversation with Attorney Bo Ryan Maverick, Brett Hamilton asked me:

Is there a title report for the property your family owns?

In addition, the "feedback" I received from (your former colleague from the Southeast Texas law firm) was;

"Since the number of potential heirs is quite numerous we cannot move forward with the suit to partition until all affidavits of heirship are completed"

Per your former colleague, once the affidavits of heirship have been completed and filed he recommended the following;

1. Suit to partition the property first – because it is a clearer kind of process (As opposed to an implied easement lawsuit where we would have to petition the court to show a number of factors
2. Then, as the suit progresses, we could add a non-compulsory joiner claim for an implied easement

Second Lead Attorney: In contrast to his former colleague, Attorney Keith Jones, the Second Lead attorney at the Southeast Texas law firm recommended a "doing it all at once" approach

In other words, if we can't get the implied easement, we will ask for the "alternative" which would be the separation

So, Step #1 will be the "letter" to Ms. Delgado to seek the "partition" The "letter' represents a pre-requisite that should be followed prior to filing the suit

The goal is to show the court that we did try to work out a deal, however an agreement could not be reached with Ms. Delgado.

The court is going to want to know, did you try to work this out? Or did you just go straight to the filing of the suit?

The response to the court from the lead attorney from the Southeast Texas firm could then be: "Well your honor, we did try to work it out, but an agreement could not be reached…So that is when we filed the suit."

The letter of demand had the force of a cannon ball fired across the bow of a warship. The reference line of the November 9, 2021 letter from the Southeast, Texas law firm read:

Re: DEMAND FOR AGREED SALE OR JUDICIAL PARTITION OF REAL PROPERTY

Subject Property – The 56 acres, more or less, of real property composed of the parcels commonly identified by Henderson Appraisal District Numbers (five parcel numbers) and the properties commonly known as (legal description of the property including five tract numbers).

The following information was presented in the history section of the letter;

History of the Subject Property

1. From 1898 to 1986, the Heirs of Rosie Edwards have owned the parcel of real property commonly identified as 56 acres of undivided interest. Rosie Edwards is Joseph Harris's great-grandmother.
2. A review of records from a March 3, 1986 (Case Number) (District Court Number) shows (a) The Harris family sued Tommie Lee Wyatt (now deceased) for trespass, (b) Mr. Wyatt counter claimed adverse possession; however before the case was submitted to the court, a settlement was reached
3. The terms of the settlement were as follows; (a) Mr. Wyatt's claim of adverse possession was dismissed, (b) the Harris family would have an undivided interest in the 56 acres, and (c) Mr. Wyatt would be awarded (tract number), (parcel number), composed of approximately 25.2-acres of land.

Tommie Lee Wyatt also owned a 50-acre tract to the west of the Subject Land.

4. Referencing the 1986 Interlocutory Judgment in a letter dated September 4, 1986 Mary A. Daffin (counsel for the Harris family) stated (a) Mr. Deuce Taylor (counsel for Mr. Wyatt) would not agree to the inclusion of language regarding partition, and (b) If the matter remained unresolved, the court would decide on how the property should be partitioned.

5. Ms. Annie Wyatt (widow of Tommy Lee Wyatt) then sold the said 25.2-acres to Cody James.

6. In 2006, Ms. Isabella Delgado purchased a 100-acre tract of land to the east of the Subject land.

7. In 2013 Mr. Cody James wrote several letters to the Harris family. The letters outlined legal steps he planned to initiate in an effort to purchase the remaining 30.8 acres.

8. Subsequently, in 2014 Mr. Cody James sold the 25.2-acres to Ms. Isabella Delgado.

9. At the time of the latter transaction, Ms. Annie Wyatt sold an additional 5-acre strip of land to Ms. Isabella Delgado.

10. The 5-acre strip of land was to the south of the Harris Family's 30.8 acres. So, Ms. Delgado's purchase of the 90-acres of land to the east (2006), 25.2-acres of land to the north (2014), and 5-acres of land to the south (2014) effectively landlocked the Harris Family's property.

11. Upon information and belief, Mr. Harris has learned that Ms. Delgado has entered onto and utilized the Harris property for purposes of hunting and has been collecting payments from third-parties for the use of the Harris' property. Ms. Delgado has not provided rental reimbursement to the Harris family for the unauthorized use of their property.

Ownership

Based on a title search using the information available, Mr. Harris has determined that ownership of the above-described 56 acres, more or less, of land is currently owned as follows:

Name	Interest
Mr. Joseph Harris (1st cousin)	19.946-acres
Mr. Walter A. Pittman Jr. (1st cousin)	3.6155-acres
Ms. Darilyn Pittman Thomas (1st cousin)	3.6155-acres
Ms. Connye Yvette Lilly Turner (1st cousin and sister to Judlyne A. Lilly)	1.80775-acres
Ms. Judlyne A. Lilly (1st cousin and sister to Connye Yvette Lilly Turner)	1.80775-acres
Ms. Isabella Delgado	25.2-acres
TOTAL	55.9925

Demand for Sale of Subject Property by Written Agreement

Mr. Harris would prefer to purchase the remainder of the Subject Property with your agreement and participation. However, if you do not cooperate, then Mr. Harris will seek a court-ordered sale. As co-owner of the Subject Property, Mr. Harris is entitled by Texas law to force the sale of the Subject Property by filing a "judicial partition" lawsuit against you.

It would be more beneficial to everyone to sell the Subject Property with your consent and written agreement because a "judicial partition" lawsuit could result in a lower sales price or require more fees. It is imperative that the Subject Property sells for the highest price possible or you and Mr. Harris risk losing all of or a significant portion of your equity in the Subject Property.

Legal Authority for Judicial Partition

"Partition" is the legal term referring to the division of real property among joint owners. The right to partition is absolute so long as the petitioning party is a joint owner of the land to be partitioned and has an equal right to possess it with the other joint owners. *Spires v. Hoover*, 466 S.W.2d 344, 346 (Tex. App. – El Paso 1971, writ ref'd n.r.e.). Mr. Harris is a joint owner with an equal right to possession of the Subject Property.

Further legal authority conclusively proving Mr. Harris's absolute right to force the sale of the Subject Property is provided by **Section 23.001 of the Texas Property Code**, which states:

A joint owner or claimant of real property or an interest in real property may compel a partition of the interest or the real property among the joint owners or claimants under this chapter and the Texas Rules of Civil Procedure.

If you refuse to voluntarily sell the Subject Property by written agreement, Mr. Harris will immediately file a lawsuit in Henderson County District Court seeking a judicially ordered partition of the Subject Property by appointing a receiver to sell the Subject Property. Please note that the costs/expenses associated with the judicial partition will be paid from sales proceeds.

Conclusion

We understand and appreciate that the process of forcing the sale of the Subject Property in this manner may not be what you desire. Therefore, it is in the best interest of you and Mr. Harris to amicably resolve any dispute as to sale of the Subject Property without judicial intervention.

The deadline for you to agree in writing to sell the Subject Property is 5:00 PM CT on Wednesday, November 24, 2021. If you fail to contact my office and/or refuse to agree in writing to agree to execute a partition deed of the Subject Property, wherein Ms. Delgado and the Harris Family will partition the Subject Property, by the aforementioned deadline, Mr. Harris will immediately file a lawsuit against you in the Henderson County District Court seeking a judicial partition of the Subject Property and he will seek to recover his reasonable and necessary attorney's fees. Again, we sincerely hope to resolve this matter by agreement and without judicial intervention.

Your prompt attention to this matter is required. Should you have any questions or comments regarding the contents of this letter, please do not hesitate to contact my office. Sincerely,

Clue: So, Step #1 will be the "letter" to Ms. Delgado to seek the "partition" The "letter' represents a pre-requisite that should be followed prior to filing the suit. The goal is to show the court that we did try to work out a deal, however an agreement could not be reached with Ms. Delgado. The court is going to want to know, did you try to work this out? Or did you just go straight to the filing of the suit? The response to the court from the lead attorney from the Southeast Texas firm could then be: "Well your honor, we did try to work it out, but an agreement could not be reached…So that is when we filed the suit." (Connect the dots).

November 16, 2021
Joe Harris Email to Lead Attorney (SE Texas firm)

Good evening Attorney Jones,

I am sure you are looking forward to taking a few days off for the Thanksgiving break.

Just touching bases to see if demand letter sent via "live service" was received by Ms. Delgado's attorney

I trust that you were able to incorporate Bo Ryan "Bo" Maverick's (Ms. Delgado's attorney) name and address into the final version (attached)

Of course, owing to COVID-related delays, the first class letters sent to Ms. Delgado's home and office – will get there when they get there

The demand letter provided Ms. Delgado with several "choices"

One of those choices was to join with the Harris Family and sell all 56 acres

if Ms. Delgado agrees to the latter "choice" and if Ms. Delgado agrees to reimburse the Harris Family for approximately $40,000 in deer hunting revenue

The friendly neighbor to the north – once told me that he was paid about $5,000 a year for leasing his 32.9-acres cow pasture to the deer hunters

Ms. Delgado has "probably" been leasing out all 56 acres of undivided interest since she acquired our 25.2-acres back in 2014.

I am available via telephone and/or email - Best Wishes,

December 2, 2021
Follow Up Email to Second Title Co. Staff Member

Good morning,

I trust you had a great Thanksgiving.

Just touching bases to see if your co-worker is getting closer to completing the encumbrance report requested on 9/29/21.

Please let me know if any additional information is required. - Best Wishes,

December 9, 2021
Summary Of Response From Second Title Co. Staff Member

- We are close to completing the Encumbrance Report
- They are just double checking some things
- The report should be ready in about a week – maybe two
- You can make the payment at that time

January 3, 2022
Follow Up Email to Second Title Co. Staff Member

Good morning, Happy New Year!

Just following up on the message that was left with your receptionist on 12/28/21

Please let your co-worker know that she is welcome to view the "Harris Family Tree" on ancestry.com

You have already been sent an invitation to view.

She can "view" via your invitation (computer) or, if you provide me with her email, I will send her an invitation via ancestry.com - Best Wishes,

January 3, 2022
Response Summary - Second Title Co. Staff Member

- He apologized for not getting back to you on this.
- He stated that he had come to an impasse because they were so far behind at the time.
- He apologized and stated he should have told me beforehand if he didn't.
- He said he could not run title because this was acreage – That he had not been taught how to do those yet and also because this was undivided interest - that was even more difficult for him.
- He stated that the other examiner would have to do this one, however he was not sure on a time frame of when she could pick this up because as he said they were a week or so behind on their own commitments plus those of other title companies that relied on their title evidence.
- So he wasn't sure if I wanted to proceed with them or to take it back to the First Title Co. of Shalene, Texas, so that they could run title where they left off since they did this title commitment for me.
- He indicated that the First Title Co. of Shalene could always just go from there and pick up - as they (Second Title Co.) would have to start back and make sure everything was added in – and concluded that they could not pick up from The First Title Co. of Shalene's commitment - as he had been told. Thank you,

January 3, 2022
Joe Harris Sent Email and Called the Second Title Co. Staff

Second Title Co. He indicated he would let his co-worker know the situation. He explained the "situation" to her – and let her know why I was reluctant to return to The First Title Co. of Shalene. I asked if any title company could run the report? He said not "any" – However, the two title companies in Shalene, Texas could run the report. He will send a follow up email tomorrow.

January 3, 2022
Joe Harris Sent Email to the Second Title Co. Staff Member's
Co-Worker (Included eleven attached files, Platt Map, etc.)

Good afternoon.

I have been communicating with [name of co-worker] since 9/29/21

It was – and still is – my understanding that he is in the process of structuring an "encumbrance report" on behalf of my family.

I have structured and filed the appropriate affidavits of heirships as well as general warranty deeds with the Henderson County Clerk's Office

I have shared several files with your co-worker – such as Henderson County recording fees for the affidavits of heirship and general warranty deeds.

In addition to the above, I have structured the Harris Family Tree

I have copy pasted below a link from ancestry.com – The link should allow you to view the Harris Family Tree

Please let me know if you require any additional information

January 5, 2022
Joe Harris Sent Email to the Original Second Title Co. Staff

Good afternoon,

I have provided [name of co-worker] with the background files needed to move forward with the encumbrance report.

I have also invited her to view the Harris Family Tree on ancestry. com

As previously noted, the Shalene, Texas property is landlocked and my family does not have the easement rights.

The family attorney is in communication with Ms. Delgado's (tenant in common) attorney regarding these matters.

The family's remaining 30.8 acres is listed as 56 acres of undivided interest

The family's legal counsel is also concerned because it appears Ms. Delgado has been leasing all 56 acres to deer hunters –

So far she has made no effort to share the deer hunting proceeds with my family.

Essentially the family is on the verge of filing a lawsuit against Ms. Delgado

When that step is taken the courts will definitely want the "owners' to be identified.

You and I have been communicating regarding this situation since 9/28/21

For a variety of reasons, I do not believe that stopping the progress you have made since 9/28/21 and returning to the First Title Co. – is a viable way to go.

Please continue to assist my family by completing the work on the encumbrance report.

Also, please keep me posted on your forward progress. - Best Wishes,

January 5, 2022
Summary of Email Response From Second Title Co. Staff

- I apologize for not getting back with you yesterday.
- I spoke with my co-worker and explained everything
- However she still does not wish to continue with this O & E Report since the First Title Co. of Shalene ran title on it.
- I apologize, I explained it to her however she does not want to move forward.

January 5, 2022
Joe Harris Email to the First Title Co. of Shalene, Texas

Good afternoon [name of staff member]

I am writing as a follow up to a conversation we had on 9/29/21.

I am requesting an encumbrance report for the following property (Legal Description of Property)

I understand that the cost of the report will be approximately $250.00

The First Title Co. of Shalene Texas prepared the attached Examiner's Notes as well as Title Commitment

I have attached additional files which should be of assistance

I will send you a link to view the Harris Family Tree – that I structured on ancestry.com

Please let me know if any additional information will be required

January 5, 2022
Joe Harris Email to the First Title Co. of Shalene Texas

Good afternoon (name of staff member)

As promised in my previous email – I am sending a link to ancestry.com

The link will allow you to view the Harris Family Tree

Please let me know if any additional information is required to complete the encumbrance report. - Sincerely,

January 6, 2022
Summary of Response From the First Title Co. of Shalene Texas

- Unfortunately we are unable to perform the work you are requesting.
- We are extremely back logged, short staffed and experiencing historic file volume.
- We are currently not accepting or processing encumbrance report orders.
- I recommend that you contact the Second Title Company of Shalene Texas (He provided the telephone number for the Second Title Co.)

January 7, 2022
Joe Harris Email to Second Lead Attorney, Southeast Texas Law Firm

Good morning Attorney Jones,

I just left two follow up messages with the First Title Co. of Shalene Texas

Mr. Brett Hamilton (First Title Co.) may not return my call today

In the meanwhile – I located a "nation-wide" service that I think can structure the encumbrance report – in a timely manner

Unfortunately, instead of the $250 value quoted by both Shalene Texas title companies – (name of online title company) appears to want to charge $250 x 5 parcels = $1,250

I will have a discussion with them regarding the $1,250 fee – However the question is – Is it OK to go forward with (name of online title company) - Best Wishes,

January 12, 2022
Joe Harris Email to Second Lead Attorney South East Texas Law Firm

Good evening Attorney Jones,

I have initiated the encumbrance/title search process

The information was entered "online" – so I am requesting the assistance of (name of online title company staff member) – as I have already provided her with background information e.g. the Heirs of Rosie chart etc. - Best Wishes,

> **Clue**: For a variety of reasons, internal decision-making on the part of The First Title Company of Shalene, Texas, as well as The Second Title Company of Shalene, Texas, made it difficult to move the process forward in a timely manner (observe but not just with the eye).

In reviewing the (name of online title company) encumbrance report (O & E report) for my late Aunt Anne (Anne P. Lilly) I discovered a handwritten deed to the Shalene, Texas, property from (volume and page number). The deed was filed for record on December 2, 1899 at 11 a.m. The deed confirms that Sallie Simpson granted Rosa Edwards rights to a specific section of her Jebediah Payne property. An excerpt from that deed is shown below.

The state of Texas know all men by County of Henderson these presents that I Sallie Simpson of the County of Henderson and State of Texas for and in the consideration of the love and affection I have for Rosa Edwards for her own use and benefit of the County of Henderson and State of Texas do grant bargain and convey and by these presents do grant bargain and convey unto the said Rosa Edwards the following tract of land lying and being in the County of Henderson, State of Texas being part of (name of survey) and being 56 acres (56 acres) to be taken out of the southwest corner of the 256 acres that was conveyed by to J.W. Duval to Green Simons June 1, 1871 and recorded in (volume and page number) Deed record of Henderson County Texas said 56 acres to be taken out of the said southwest corner in a form and manner as will be make it a fair tract of land and to be selected as to boundaries by said Rosa Edwards and field notes to be recorded by her as shown as so selected as part of this deed.

BEGINNING at the stake in South boundary line of said survey, it being the Southeast corner of 50-acres surveyed by Wm. Simpson from which a red oak 10 in. dia. X vrs. North 50 West 5-5/10 brs., another 4 in. x brs. North 86 West 3-6/10 vrs.;

THENCE East 287-2/10 vrs. To stake from which a red oak 5 in. dia. brs. South 64 – ½ West 3 – 4/10 vrs., another brs. South 76 East 2 – 5/10 vrs.;

THENCE North 20 West 1097 vrs. To stake in Eiglebiger's South boundary line from which a double red oak 12 in. brs. South 9 West 5-6/10 vrs.;

THENCE West with said line 287-2/10 vrs. To Wm. Simpson's Northeast corner from which a sweet gum 8 in. brs. South 61 West 1-4/10 vrs.;

THENCE South 20 West 1097 vrs. To Beginning: the same containing 56 acres of land and being the same land as described in a deed dated August 2, 1898 from Sallie Simpson to Rosa Edwards Recorded of Record in (volume and page number) et seq., Deed Records of Henderson County, Texas

Clue: The terms of the 1986 decision specified that, until the metes and bounds of the property were determined by a survey team, the property would be held in a kind of tenants in common status. That meant Isabella Delgado had the right to roam throughout all 56 acres and so did my family. Paradoxically Ms. Delgado had access to all the property, my family did not. The court did not, however, grant Tommy Lee Wyatt, and subsequently Ms. Delgado, the right to lease the family's 30.8 acres to the deer hunters without our permission (think backward).

Clue: A review of letters associated with the 1986 Interlocutory Judgment proceedings revealed that several parties suspected the 25.3-acres had been illegally acquired from the heirs of Rosie. The foundation for this concern is presented below (think backward)

In an effort to obtain a better appreciation for the history linked to the Shalene, Texas, property, I spent a considerable amount of time reviewing letters and documents related to the 1986 Interlocutory Judgment. As previously noted, it described the property as 56 acres of undivided interest. At one point all 56 acres belonged to the heirs of Rosie. However, after the 1986 judgment, only 30.8 acres still belonged to the family. The other 25.3-acres was awarded to the late Mr. Wyatt. Mr. Wyatt's widow then sold the acreage to an attorney, who then sold it to Ms. Delgado (for an undisclosed amount). During the latter transaction, Ms. Delgado also purchase a five-acre strip to the south of the family's property. Ms. Delgado already owned 90 acres to the east of the family property.

August 10, 1979:
Letter to James Pittman From a Law Firm Representing Him

In July of 1978, we received correspondence from Andy Kinkaid advising of the manner in which his father acquired a portion of the

56 acre tract in 1936. He also expressed concern about the intentions of a Mr. Wyatt to whom his interest was sold.

The chain of title subsequently received from Henderson Abstract Company also showed two other sales to Mr. Wyatt, one in 1971 by the Remington's and the other in 1973 by Levi Jackson. The Kinkaid – Wyatt sale would account for that portion of the tract inherited by Green and Annie Edwards. The chain of title, however, does not reveal how or through whom Levi Jackson acquired his interest, or whether this person is an *Heir of Rosie* and Hector Edwards. The heirship chart notes that Mattie Jackson, an heir, had no children, so it would appear that Levi acquired his interest by purchase. I am particularly concerned about this conveyance by Jackson, since it may be the instrument under which Wyatt intends to assert title to the entire tract.

I recently spoke to Andy Kinkaid who emphasized the reputation of Wyatt for taking land in the area. He also noted that he knew the exact location of this tract.

From the heirship chart, it would appear that you, Mrs. Williams and your other brothers and sisters own an undivided one-fifth or 11.2 acres of the 56-acre tract. According to Andy Kinkaid, the land probably has a value of between $500 and $1,000 per acre, making your family's interest worth between $5,600 and $11,200.

Two things need to be determined at this time. First, whether Wyatt has on record an instrument showing he is the owner of the entire 56 acres. Second, whether Wyatt has fenced in or otherwise asserted his dominion and control over the entire tract by grazing cattle or otherwise. If either of these events has occurred, legal action needs to be taken against him immediately. I cannot at this time advise as to the likely outcome of any such suit. I would advise, however, that he would most likely raise as a defense both the three-year and the five-year statutes of limitations.

I indicated in our telephone conversation of August 3 that I probably can travel to Shalene at sometime within the next two to three weeks to look at the land in question and to review the deed records. It has since occurred to me that it may be more expedient in terms of time and expense to obtain copies of the deeds by mail and for you and I to arrange to visit the land at your first available weekend. Mr. Kinkaid has indicated a willingness to point it out to us.

In light of the previous fees you have paid for this initial investigation, I anticipate no further charges other than a seventeen cents per mile charge for travel to Shalene to complete this investigation.

Please let me hear from you as soon as you have had an opportunity to review this letter.

Very Truly Yours

> **Clue:** As early as August 10, 1979, an attorney retained by the Pittmans raised the following concerns: "The chain of title subsequently received from the Second Title Company of Shalene, Texas also showed two other sales to Mr. Wyatt, one in 1971 by the Remington's and the other in 1973 by Levi Jackson. The Kinkaid - Wyatt sale would account for that portion of the tract inherited by Green and Annie Edwards (think backward)

> **Clue:** The chain of title, did not reveal how or through whom Levi Jackson acquired his interest, or whether this person was an Heir of Rosie and Hector Edwards. The heirship chart noted that Mattie Jackson, an heir, had no children, so it appeared that Levi acquired his interest by purchase. The attorney was particularly concerned about the conveyance by Jackson, since it may have been the instrument under which Wyatt intended to assert title to the entire tract" (always be a skeptic)

May 10, 1982:
Letter to Albert C. Williams (Heir of Rosie) from a law firm representing the family

I need your help and/or the assistance of some other members of the family. As you are familiar, our investigation revealed your Aunt Mattie E. Jackson died while married to Lee Jackson. Lee

Jackson died, and so far as our side of the family shows, he had no children.

The investigation in Shalene shows after the death of Aunt Mattie he in fact married Ludie Jackson. She is still living. Lee and Ludie had one (1) child, L.V. Jackson. When he died his entire interest descended to his son, L.V.

Tommy Lee Wyatt has come up with this deed from Levi Jackson. His mother states L.V.'s name is not Levi and he has not adopted the name of Levi nor has he ever been called Levi. Based upon this information we believe that the proposed deed is from a person not in the chain of title, or is a pure forgery.

The problem we have however, is L.V. is lying in a "coma" in Galveston Hospital with a brain tumor. Additionally, his wife Maude Jackson is most uncooperative. Currently his mother Ludie is in Galveston visiting her brother Allen Dial.

This letter is to solicit the free and voluntary cooperation of either or all of them. Additionally, we cannot partition the land, obtain a clear title and settle the lawsuit unless we have all of the necessary parties joined. L.V.'s wife is a necessary party.

While this letter is directed to you, by a copy I am letting my other clients know of the situation with the hope they will proceed to act, or assist you in this chore.

Mr. Dial's telephone number is (telephone number) and Mrs. Maude Jackson's is (telephone number). If they do not cooperate we will be required to sue them, plus take their deposition. Both are costly but additionally so time consuming when they (L.V.) has the most to gain.

Please let me hear from you shortly since this case has been reset for trial the week beginning July 19, 1982.

Very Truly Yours

Clue: The investigation in Shalene showed that after the death of Aunt Mattie he in fact married Ludie Jackson. She was still living. Lee and Ludie had one (1) child, L.V. Jackson. When Lee died his entire interest descended to his son, L.V. (think backward)

Clue: Tommy Lee Wyatt produced a deed that was signed by a Levi Jackson. His mother stated L.V.'s name was not Levi and he had not adopted the name of Levi nor had he ever been called Levi. Based upon this information the attorney believed that the proposed deed was from a person not in the chain of title, or was a pure forgery. (always be a skeptic)

Clue: The problem was L.V. was lying in a "coma" in a Galveston Hospital with a brain tumor. Additionally, his wife Maude Jackson was most uncooperative. Also at the time, his mother Ludie was in Galveston visiting her brother Allen Dial. (observe – but not just with the eye)

Clue: The attorney affirmed that they could not partition the land, obtain a clear title and settle the lawsuit unless they had all of the necessary parties joined and L.V.'s wife was a necessary party (think backward)

May 13, 1982:
Handwritten note on Geraldine P. Wooten stationery to family

Hi Family Members,

We are attaching copies of our latest correspondence from the attorney. The letter to Albert C. Williams is interesting. It's about our old "Uncle Lee." As far as we know he had no children. Someone is trying to prove he did. A.C. Williams is Louise's son (Louise was Dorothea's daughter) - Maude and Jim

Clue: According to Geraldine P. Wooten (Aunt Geri) "It's about our old 'Uncle Lee.' As far as we know he had no children. Someone is trying to prove he did." (always be a skeptic)

March 19, 1986:
First Two Paragraphs of Letter From Maudell P. Williams to Family Revisited

"This letter is to inform you that our family <u>WON</u> the court case involving the property in Shalene, Texas. That's great, isn't it?!

On Monday, March 3, 1986, Jim, Anne and I went to Shalene, Texas where Attorney Mary Daffin represented us. She was super! We drove up from Houston early Monday morning with the intention of being in court only one day. We ended up having to spend two nights and being in court 2 ½ days. After hearing both sides, Edwards/ Pittman vs. Tommy Lee Wyatt, the Judge agreed that we indeed were the rightful *heirs* to this property. We answered questions on the stand to the best of our ability and also entered into evidence a large notebook with old letters, receipts and cancelled checks proving our claim.

The amount of land involved was 56 acres. We won all of that back but 3 parcels. Those were given to Tommy Lee Wyatt some time ago by Uncle Buddy (Greed Edwards). That was my mother's brother. The other was given away by George Martin, Aunt Rebecca's son, and someone named Levi Jackson gave his part also to Tommy Lee Wyatt. So we get all but those 3 shares. After this land is surveyed, we'll know exactly how many acres we'll have proper and clear title to.

> **Clue:** According to Aunt Maude, "The amount of land involved was 56 acres. We won all of that back but 3 parcels. Those were given to Tommy Lee Wyatt some time ago by Uncle Buddy (Green Edwards). That was my mother's brother. The other was given away by George Martin, Aunt Rebecca's son, and someone named Levi Jackson gave his part also to Tommy Lee Wyatt. (think backward)

Clue: Also according to Aunt Maude, "So we get all but those 3 shares. After this land is surveyed, we'll know exactly how many acres we'll have proper and clear title to." (think backward)

Clue: The 25.3-acres that Mr. Wyatt received as part of the 1986 Interlocutory Judgement proceedings consisted of three 8.43-acre parcels. Mr. Wyatt was able to show that 16.87 acres were either sold or transferred to him by the heirs of Rosie. The remaining 8.43-acres were linked to Levi Jackson. It appears that the attorney representing the Pittman's' interest advised to not dispute the Levi Jackson deed. This is evidenced by the fact that the name Levi Jackson and not L.V. Jackson was listed on page 8 of the Plaintiff's Exhibit 1: Heirs of Rosie (eliminate the inessential)

As a follow up to the May 10, 1982, letter from a family attorney to my now deceased aunts and uncle, I elected to conduct additional research. My goal was to assist in understanding the late Levy Jackson's role in the 1986 proceedings. Was the inclusion of the deed from Levy Jackson simply a ploy utilized by the late Mr. Wyatt to steal the *heirs'* property? As noted in the 1982 letter, the operating assumptions were the deed is from a person not in the chain of title or is a pure forgery

A review of records in the ancestry.com Harris Family Tree reveals that L.V. Jackson had a son named L.H. Jackson as well as a sister Ruth Farrington. Perhaps one or more of the latter parties could have shed light on the L.V. versus Levi "name" controversy.

Clue: A review of records in the ancestry.com Harris Family Tree revealed that L.V. Jackson had a wife Maude Jackson, mother Ludie Dials, son L.V. Jackson, Brother Geran Revenell, adopted sister Ruth Farrington, 3 uncles, 4 sister-in-laws, and 2 brothers-in-law. Perhaps in lieu of the wife and mother, one or more of the remaining parties could have shed light on whether the deed signed by Levi Jackson was indeed a forgery (think backward)

Clue: In reference to the 25.3-acres that the Pittman's relinquished to the late Mr. Wyatt, it appeared he did provide evidence that the following Heirs of Rosie sold their interest in the property to him; (a) Green and Annie Edwards (8.43-acres) and (b) George Martin (8.43-acres). Interest for the remaining 8.43- acres was allegedly provided by Levi Jackson (think backward)

As previously noted, on October 21, 2021, I signed the second of two "Agreements for Legal Services" with the Southeast Texas law firm. I then discussed with the lead attorney the feasibility of comparing Levi Jackson's signature on the 1986 deed to his signature on his draft card as well as his driver's license. I was able to download L.V. Jackson's draft card from ancestry.com. I then contacted the Texas Department of Public Safety and requested a copy of L.V. Jackson's driver's license. A copy of the letter to the Texas Department of Public Safety is shown below.

February 7, 2022:
Joe Harris Letter to the Texas Department of Public Safety

Good afternoon all,

My name is Joe Harris - I am requesting a copy of a driver's license for L.V. Jackson –

L.V. Jackson was born on September 10, 1923 – in Shalene, Henderson, Texas USA

L.V. Jackson died on May 8, 1982 – in Texas City, Galveston County Texas, Galveston, Texas USA

L.V. Jackson was the stepson of my grand aunt

This fact can be verified by viewing the Harris Family Tree on ancestry.com (an invitation to view can be sent upon request)

L.V. Jackson signed a deed on July 19, 1973

The deed was recorded in Henderson, Texas on August 2, 1973

A copy of L.V. Jackson's 1973 driver's license would be preferred

However copies of any and all L.V. Jackson driver's licenses would be acceptable –

I am attempting to reconcile the signature on the 07/19/1973 deed with the signature on his driver's license

That is because the deed was signed by Levi Jackson – and it is my understanding that the signature on the deed should have been L.V. Jackson – Thank You

February 25, 2022:
Texas Department of Public Safety Email to Joe Harris

RE: Public Information Request for driver license information for L.V. Jackson (7 digit public information number)

Mr. Harris:

The Department received your above-referenced request on February 7, 2022. The Department has conducted a good faith search for any and all information related to your request and has not been able to locate any responsive records with the information you provided. If you have any questions regarding this request, please submit them in writing via email to OGC.Webmaster@dps.texas.gov or via mail to the address in the letterhead. Thank you.

Cordially,

Clue: The response was in keeping with a previous communication received from the Texas Department of Public Safety. The representative mentioned that the department did not issue driver's licenses to individuals with initials. My concern, however, was that it was highly unlikely that L.V. Jackson did not have a driver's license (always be a skeptic)

Clue: Under the advice and guidance of legal counsel. I reached a conclusion that was probably similar to that reached by my late aunts and uncle. It did not seem worthwhile to continue this particular line of investigation over what probably would amount to about 8.43 acres of land (eliminate the inessential)

After communications were resumed with the Southeast Texas law firm, the lead attorney suggested that Connye Turner (*first cousin*) consider switching parcels with me so that the 15.4-acres that were assigned to me via the encumbrance reports, would be all together. The Platt Map shows Darilyn Thomas and James Pittman Jr. with Parcel A (7.7-acres), me with Parcel B (7.7-acres), Connye Turner and Judlyne A. Lilly with Parcel C (7.7-acres) and me with Parcel D (7.7-acres). However, Connye Turner, first agreed to the switch and then changed her mind the next day, ruling instead in favor of selling all 56 acres.

After I shared the family decision to sell all 56 acres with the lead attorney, there have been a series of delays in the filing of the case. The lead attorney first cited the departure of a fellow staff member from the firm (and his need to address the pending cases that his staff member left), then illness, and then an additional excessive and rather pressing workload. More recently, the attorney has gone dark on me, and has not responded to my infrequent emails requesting a status update. So, as of August 2022 (nine months later), the "Demand for Agreed Sale or Judicial Partition of Real Property" dated November 9, 2021, appeared to have temporarily lost traction and stalled out.

At that point I had already spent approximately $17,000 on Shalene, Texas–related activities. The proposed lawsuit would cost an additional $10,000 to $14,000. The latter value would be dependent upon any counter-measures Ms. Delgado might take.

Short of implementing a revenue-generating plan for the property, the only way for me to regain funds expended was through the sale of the property. In addition, I set up a Pittman Family Fund and encouraged all family members to assist with on-going expenditures. I also shared with the *first cousins* year one and year two projections. These projections indicated that if we worked together, we could manage the on-going costs for taxes and maintenance, as well as security measures. Those measures would include on-ground patrols as well as a camera relay system designed to ward off potential trespassers. The financial projections showed that as a 50 percent owner, I would shoulder 50 percent of the latter costs.

Unfortunately, the *first cousins* were simply not in favor of retaining the property. Other than James Pittman, Jr. (who contributed a rather substantial amount), as well as Walter Pittman Jr. (member at large), and Connye Lilly Turner, most family members have refrained from contributing money to the on-going Shalene, Texas, dilemma.

> **Clue**: At that point I had already spent approximately $17,000 on Shalene, Texas–related activities. The proposed lawsuit would cost an additional $10,000 to $14,000. The latter value would be dependent upon any counter-measures Ms. Delgado might take. (Notice the finer details, not just the glaringly obvious)

Clue: Short of implementing a revenue-generating plan for the property, the only way for me to regain funds expended was through the sale of the property. In addition, I set up a Pittman Family Fund and encouraged all family members to assist with on-going expenditures. I also shared with the *first cousins* year one and year two projections. These projections indicated that if we worked together we could manage the on-going costs for taxes, maintenance, as well as security measures (Connect the dots. Connect observation A to observation B to observation C and so on)

Perhaps the key to getting the lawsuit back on track would be to (a) revisit previous buyout discussions with my *first cousins*, and (2) shift the focus from a suit to sell all 56 acres (equivalent to a hail Mary pass) to a suit to partition the 56 acres. Considering that Ms. Delgado's attorneys would (a) probably oppose the sale of all 56 acres and (b) the latter action would result in an increase in legal fees to be paid by the plaintiff (Joe Harris). Therefore, I suspect that the suit to partition approach would represent the path of least resistance.

The dilemma was that if I agreed to force the sale of all 56 acres, we would lose our claim to the legacy of generational wealth. However, if we sold all 56 acres, I stood to receive as much as $61,500. And so, the process of weighing and balancing the three options had left me conflicted. One thing was for sure: Ms. Delgado was not going to simply roll over and allow the sale of her 25.3 acres without a fight. That fight would probably increase the initial $10,000 attorney fee to $14,000 or more. In addition, the time frame for a court-ordered resolution to the matter would probably be extended.

On the one hand, my personal preference had always been to retain the legacy of generational wealth. However, to do so would mean that, unless a revenue-generating plan was implemented, or I sold the property, I would have no way of regaining past expenditures. In addition, as the sole owner, I would also be faced with a minimum amount of $52,500 in on-going Shalene, Texas-related costs.

On the other hand, my *first cousins*, owing to other priorities, were steadfast in their desire to sell the property. As a result, they simply were not interested in a suit to partition. The latter option would entail sharing the upkeep and maintenance costs associated with the retention. As previously noted, the *first cousins* were also opposed to the concept of switching parcels – which would have allowed me an opportunity to position my 15.4-acres in a side by side manner. It was at that point that I scheduled a Zoom Meeting. A primary purpose of the meeting was to explore in real time potential areas of agreement/disagreement and attempt to broker a mutually agreed upon compromise regarding a future course of action.

August 14, 2022
Announcement

From: Joe Harris
To: Connye Y. Turner, Judlyne A. Lilly, James Pittman, Darilyn Pittman, and Walter A. Pittman
Subject: Joe Harris is inviting you to a scheduled Zoom meeting.
Topic: Shalene, Texas
Time: Aug 16, 2022 10:00 AM Pacific Time (US and Canada)
Join Zoom Meeting
https://us05web.zoom.us/j/89613607185?pwd=VUpjeUJxWHhqUF BWSCtMbG1Teko0UT09
Meeting ID: 896 1360 7185
Passcode: 24R7AA - Best Wishes,

August 15, 2022
Email From Joe Harris to Invited Zoom Meeting Attendees

Good evening all,

I am looking forward to seeing you again during the Tuesday August 16, 2022 Zoom meeting

That evening I received the following text message, followed by an email from Connye.

Connye Yvette Turner: Joe, Judlyne and I want Option 3 (decision to sell to Joe)

I did attempt to call Connye (twice) on Thursday, August 11, 2022 – However she did not have an opportunity to call me back. So I called her again on Sunday, August 14, 2022. She couldn't talk to me but asked if I had received a call from Judlyne (I had not). So she said she would remind Judlyne to call me. So far I had not had an opportunity to talk to Judlyne.

If I had a chance to talk to them I would have explained that the $14,000 buyout value was a "dummy' value, e.g. a holding place for future discussion.

It appeared that Connye and Judlyne – minus the discussion – had selected Option 3 – and assumed that the $14,000 "dummy" value was a "done deal."

The Agenda for the Zoom Meeting was Option 1 or Option 2 or Option 3 – To be followed by some sort of "discussion."

I had attached three (3) buy-out scenarios that could be used for the "discussion," which – so far – had not taken place with Connye and Judlyne

The Zoom Meeting would be limited to 40 minutes – so I was hoping we could be as efficient as possible with the time.

If more discussion was required, we could still do so on a one on one basis – or schedule another Zoom Meeting

In the meanwhile – I had focused on Option 3 and attached three (3) Option 3 buy-out scenarios

I put some elbow work into Scenario 1 back on June 15, 2022 – however I didn't think it was a realistic way to go

Scenario 2 was the best option (e.g. repay Connye and Darilyn all the money they had paid in taxes over the years) – However, one of the *first cousins* had already mentioned she was expecting more money.

Scenario 3 – which was what Connye and Judlyne elected (without discussing the matter with me) – was not a good deal – e.g.

in addition to paying them for all the taxes they had paid over the years – Connye, Judlyne and Darilyn would remove themselves from this entire Shalene, Texas situation and receive over $4,000 in profit for their trouble

So now let's actually do what – so far has not been done – Lets Discuss! These matters and not just send a one (1) line text message and/or email –

Best Wishes,

August 19, 2022 -
Joe Harris Email to Southeast Texas Second Lead Attorney

Good afternoon Attorney Jones,

I have decided to select the "suit to partition" option

It is OK to move forward at this time with the "suit to partition"

Ms. Delgado has been leasing out our portion of the land for at least the past nine (9) years

So, $5,000/year times 9 = $45,0000 – that I believe she owes the family

In addition, please include a request for the *easement* rights via the shorter route from the County Road

I called Mr. Fontenette last night – and he is still willing to grant the *easement* rights – along the outer edge of his cow pasture (the longer route)

I did my best to discuss the future direction of the pending lawsuit with my *first cousins*

I scheduled a Zoom Meeting, however, the key decision-makers did not participate

I left voice messages for Connye Turner and Judlyne A. Lilly – however my calls were not returned

I conducted a follow up teleconference with two (2) of the decision-makers Darilyn P. Thomas and James Pittman Jr. (brother and sister)

James Pittman Jr. transferred his interest to his sister Darilyn P. Thomas – However the "encumbrance report" still shows him as a co-owner with Darilyn P. Thomas

Darilyn Thomas indicated that she wished to retain her 7.7-acres – and stand in court with me –

So far Darilyn has done a great job of paying the annual $200 (approximately) tax bill

However, I have concerns about the degree to which she would be willing to prioritize one fourth of the costs of projected expenditures such as (1) a survey team, (2) a fence, a bridge etc.

And so, for a number of reasons, I will follow up with Darilyn and – once again – attempt to buy her out

Although they did not participate in the Zoom, and – so far have not made themselves available for a teleconference

Connye Yvette Turner and Judlyne A. Lilly (sisters) sent me a text message (followed by an email) and indicated that they wish me to buy them out for a total amount of $7,000

That is about $2,000 more than I believe they are entitled to – however, in light of the history of internal discussions with them – I plan to honor their request for $7,000

I trust you can move forward with the "suit to partition" – and that if/when I complete the general warranty deed + "recording" process with Connye Y. Turner and Judlyne A. Lilly the language of the lawsuit can be "amended" to reflect any changes in final ownership.

Please let me know if any additional information is required - Best wishes,

For a brief moment, I paused and reflected upon what could be described as *the still small voices in my head*. The voices represented the wide range of advice/guidance received from various parties through-out the Shalene, Texas journey. For example,

December 2, 2013
Attorney Franklin Peters - Practiced Law Near the Florida Panhandle (upon learning that my first cousins had decided to go in a different direction)

It certainly is. I am going to miss working on this case…

April 25, 2018
Ava Nelson, Shalene, Texas Real Estate Agent

At what point will yawl consider getting yawl selves an attorney?

April 27, 2018
Shalene, Texas Real Estate Attorney

Essentially I am talking about going through the paper work to determine (a) implied easement in the chain of title or (b) direct easement in the chain of title. Or to see if there are grounds in the paperwork for an easement by necessity. My retainer would be $15,000. The whole thing could easily run $20,000. So it's not worth it! Now you have a good day, you hear?

May 29, 2018
Summary of Email From Houston, Texas-Based First Cousin to Joe Harris

According to my *first cousin*, she and her sister did not agree that I would pay $30.000 etc. to a lawyer and be reimbursed when and if the property sells.

Adding that they agreed that I would negotiate the best price I could get from anyone who wanted to buy the property. According to her, they were not interested in dealing with lawyers.

July 9, 2018
First Cousin

Thank you Joe. It looks good but I'm a little confused about the "worth" of the property versus the "sale price" of the property

The property is valued at over $82,000 however, the selling price will be $24,000 (cash)

July 9, 2018
Attorney Frank Peters (Florida Panhandle)

Let me read any contract before it is signed

July 12, 2018
Attorney Frank Peters (Florida Panhandle - He agreed to participate in an advisory role only)

I am not real fond of annuities – in principal. But if that is your choice of investment/retirement planning, then I see nothing wrong

July 13, 2018
First Cousin

Joe, I really appreciate everything you have done, but after all we all have gone through with this property and the shady deal the attorneys are giving us. Nobody has any money to continue with all the fees involved, it'll just be to costly for most of us. I would rather just take my $200 or $300's and end this thing, because there are too many options we could do as a family, but without all participants agreeing on one thing we will never get it straight. So let's just call it what it is, OVER.. I Hate to say that but I would like to sell the property and be done....

Sorryyyyyyyyyyy...

July 13, 2018
First Cousin

I agree with (name of first cousin). Let's take the little bit of money and run screaming from this

July 16, 2018
First Cousin

Joe, as discussed recently, I will defer any money assigned to me.

July 23, 2018
Attorney Frank Peters (Florida Panhandle) -

Subject: RE: (name of investment group)

So how does it compare to the former offer? It doesn't appear that it allows for the reservation of minerals

July 24, 2018
Attorney Frank Peters (Florida Panhandle)

Subject: RE: (name of investment group)

You sure you don't want a second career as a land man?

August 26, 2018
Texas-Based First Cousins

The three of us are requesting that you cease all calls until someone calls you. Then you can notify us

August 26, 2018
Attorney Frank Peters (Florida Panhandle)

This is taking on a life of its own is it not?

September 27, 2018
Attorney Frank Peters (Florida Panhandle)

Subject: RE: Joe's Response to Darilyn's 9/27/18 Inquiry
What a family saga!

January 26, 2019
Attorney Frank Peters (Florida Panhandle)

RE: Joe Harris regarding Shalene, Texas Property
Getting an agreement in a situation like yours usually requires a miracle unless the payday is big

February 18, 2019
Attorney Frank Peters (Florida Panhandle)

Subject: RE: Decision to Retain the Shalene, Texas Property
Big plans, but doable. I have been monitoring this matter for Joe and he has really put out the effort. It is now the time for all to pitch in as they can.
I am admitted in Texas, but I am more conversant with real

property law in Florida – and they differ. You need to engage a lawyer on the ground in that county to monitor things ongoing - Good Luck, and keep me in the loop

Subject: RE: Option to Purchase Agreement Item #1
You and I are in the same bracket – over 70, but I will take helicopters as long as it isn't a (name of company)l! My former colleagues in Texas tell me that affidavits of heirship border on malpractice for the lawyer, because anyone can say anything. What is the alternative – I don't know.

March 26, 2019
Attorney Frank Peters (Florida Panhandle)

Subject: RE: Draft Cease & Desist Letter
Looks good to me

March 26, 2019
Attorney Frank Peters (Florida Panhandle)

Subject: RE: Draft Cease & Desist Letter
If there is such a thing as reincarnation, I plan to return as either a surveyor or a court reporter. Those two sets of folks are never out of work. Certified letter is probably not necessary, but an incessant stream of phone calls might work. Check the surrounding count seat towns if you hit a brick wall.

April 1, 2019
Attorney Frank Peters (Florida Panhandle)

The only way to know for sure would be to examine the court file. My guess is that they have been photocopied to either microfilm or fiche and it would require an on-site examination at the court house.

July 2, 2019
Attorney Frank Peters (Florida Panhandle)

What problem are you having with that firm?

Your letter is concise and to the point. I haven't examined the chain so I really have no opinion on ownership, but you did have it researched as I recall. Perhaps I can help.

August 1, 2019
Attorney Frank Peters (Florida Panhandle)

I hate to see you go it solo in court over a property issue. Is there no-one in East Texas who can be of assistance?

May 4, 2021
Attorney Danny Wilks (First Lead Attorney North Texas Law Firm)

You really need to get in there with a survey team so you can see what you are getting yourself into

September 14, 2021
Attorney Frank Peters (Florida Panhandle)

Subject: RE: Shalene Texas Property - Feedback From North Texas Law Firm Pending
This has been a long haul; is there a light at the end of the tunnel – or just another train?

September 15, 2021
Attorney Frank Peters (Florida Panhandle)

Subject: RE: Shalene Texas Property - Feedback From North Texas Law Firm Pending – Joseph Harris Response
Considering your effort on this property, when did you have the time to write another book. I look forward to the publication.

September 27, 2021
Julius Johnston (Second Lead Attorney North Texas Law Firm)

I don't like to see my clients spend an excessive amount of money and not achieve the kind of outcome they are expecting. In other words, the partition will not get a result you want. Adding, even if you were able to get Ms. Delgado out, your problems with her are not going to go away. (Unfortunately the Second Attorney did not elaborate).

I encourage you to step away from any emotional attachment to the property. In a court of law emotional components count for nothing. For example, argument like we have had the property since 1898 and Ms. Delgado just acquired her property in 1996 and 2014 respectively. Or your family doesn't like her because of the aggressive manner in which she has attempted to gain control of all of the property.

November 10, 2021
Attorney Frank Peters (Florida Panhandle)

Subject: RE: Demand Letter For Shalene, Texas Property
Very Good letter. It tells it like it is. I hope the people cooperate to save everyone a bunch of money.

January 5, 2022
Staff Member, Second Title Company of Shalene, Texas

I apologize for not getting back with you yesterday
I spoke with my co-worker and explained everything
However she still does not wish to continue with this O& E
Report since the First Title Co. of Shalene Texas ran title on it
I apologize, I explained it to her however she does not want to move forward

January 6, 2022
Staff Member, First Title Company of Shalene, Texas

Unfortunately we are unable to perform the work you are Requesting - We are extremely back logged, short staffed and experiencing historic file volume - We are currently not accepting or processing encumbrance report orders.

I recommend that you contact the Second Title Company of Shalene Texas (telephone number provided)

January 13, 2022
Attorney Frank Peters (Florida Panhandle)

Subject: RE: Happy New Year + Update Shalene, Texas
This appears to have become a full-time pursuit for you. I appreciate the updates. The goal may be in sight!

In contrast to the comments made by the Second Lead Attorney from the law firm based in North Texas, on May 3, 2022 the lead attorney from the Southeast Texas firm stated;

May 3, 2022
Teleconference Attorney Keith Jones (Second Lead Attorney SE Law Firm)

Second Lead Attorney: Yes it is possible to force the sale of all 56 acres. However, given the amount of land involved, there is no need to sell all 56 acres.

Joe Harris: In other words, he was suggesting that perhaps a suit to partition, would be the preferred way to go. Especially since the latter path would allow the family to retain 30.8- acres.

Second Lead Attorney: You should consider buying out the *first cousins*. If the buyout concept is not feasible, you should consider switching parcels with one of the *first cousins*. The latter step would allow you to retain 15.4-acres.

Ms. Delgado will file some sort of motion against the forced sale of all 56 acres. The latter motion will probably result in an increase from the $10,000 value originally quoted, to approximately $14,000.

Chapter Five

On August 9, 2022, I signed a second "agreement for legal services" with the Southeast Texas-based law firm.

Scope of Services. Represent Client in partition litigation opposite cotenants

Fees and Expenses. For the Firm to represent you, the Firm will require a $10,000 deposit.

August 9, 2022
Joe Harris Teleconference with Keith Jones (the Second Lead Attorney)

Second Lead I will send you (Joe Harris) the agreement for legal services today.
Attorney: Joe Harris should reach out to the *first cousins* regarding the sale of all 56 acres versus suit to partition matter. "Whichever way you (as a family) want to take this will be fine. "Whichever way

the family decides e.g. suit to sell it all versus partition – we can handle it. So, you can acquire your family's interest – whatever you want – Suit to partition, versus sell it – Or acquire the interest first – It will be up to you – Some routes will take longer than others – owing to the unique circumstances – So the agreement will represent the retention of services. If we sell etc. If you decide to retain – The good thing is you will have the ability to sell – Have a great day, talk to soon – We should be OK in terms of the filing of the lawsuit timeline

Me: Basically I want to retain the property – However, given the rather lengthy history of problems associated with the property + other priorities - the *first cousins* simply wanted **OUT**. Question: (Joe Harris) "Do we have one (1) day or two (2) days to reply? If so, I need to set up a Zoom, or conduct one on one teleconferences"

Second Lead Attorney: Take as long as you like to let me know how you wish to proceed –

> **Clue**: Joe Harris should reach out to the *first cousins* regarding the sale of all 56 acres versus suit to partition matter. "Whichever way you (as a family) want to take this will be fine. "Whichever way the family decides e.g. suit to sell it all versus partition – we can handle it. So, you can acquire your family's interest – whatever you want – Suit to partition, versus sell it – Or acquire the interest first – It will be up to you – Some routes will take longer than others – owing to the unique circumstances – So the agreement will represent the retention of services. If you sell etc. If you decide to retain – The good thing is you will have the ability to sell – Have a great day, talk to soon – We should be OK in terms of the filing of the lawsuit timeline (Connect the dots. Connect observation A to observation B to observation C and so on)

August 16, 2022
Joe Harris Email to Judlyne A. Lilly

Good afternoon Judlyne,

Thank you for the follow up

That was the first Zoom session that I "conducted" –

As always, I learned a few things – like maybe I should pay Zoom "more money" in case the session goes longer than the 40 minutes of "free Zoom" allocated

It is always good to see close family members – Zoom seems to make get togethers more convenient for everyone

I did receive Connye's communications regarding "Option 3"

As you can imagine, I am already stretched out "financially" – As of today I believe I have spent approximately $27,000.00 on the Shalene, Texas situation ....

100 percent ownership will probably move me up over the $50,000.00 mark

So my question to you and Connye is

Is there a "buy-out" compromise point (could be a half-way mark) between the $4,251.78 + $230.64 taxes + $100 = $4,582.42 (includes $1,000 in legal fees paid by Connye) and the $7,000 figure Connye referenced in the past and is once again referencing?

I did conduct a teleconference with Darilyn after the Zoom session

However, I am still not sure about her final position on all of this –

I plan to follow up with her as soon as possible - Best Wishes,

August 20, 2022 -
Joe Harris Email to Connye Yvette Turner and Judlyne A. Lilly

Good afternoon Connye and Judlyne

Judlyne thank you for the follow up call – I did receive the voice mail you left this morning

Now that I know how to "Zoom" – I am sure I will have future opportunities to interact via Zoom

However, next time I will probably sign up for one of the membership plans –

A membership "plan" allows parties to talk longer than the 40 minutes set aside for a "free" Zoom

I have attached the general warranty deed –

Since you two have not had an opportunity to respond Yes or No to my proposal for a "compromise" –

I assume you would prefer that I pay the larger sum of $7,000.00

I know that you two are not "geographically" situated near one another – so,

Option 1

One suggestion is that either one of you get the "notary" component started and then FedEx etc. the original to the other

So that the latter party can sign and have their signature notarized

Option 2

Each of you complete the Signature + notary process and forward the original to me (without the other parties signature etc.)

Which means I would have the same GWD registered twice with Henderson County

Just let me know what will work for you

I mentioned (in an email) to the lead attorney that your Mom's property had not been transferred

Since he did not respond – I did the best I could to structure the GWD – with the information I have – Hopefully the Henderson County clerks will accept.

Please give me a call, or send an email/text if you have any additional questions

Best Wishes,

August 20, 2022
Joe Harris Email to Darilyn P. Thomas and James Pittman, Jr.

Good afternoon Darilyn and Jimmy,

As requested, I sent a general warranty deed to Connye and Judlyne.

Just in case – I have also - attached a general warranty deed – for you and Jimmy

I have had several "buy-out" conversations with Darilyn

Connye and Judlyne have both selected Option 3 – the buy- out option-

I think I can address the Shalene, Texas situation in a more timely , efficient, and cost effective manner – If I go it alone

I am offering you a total of $7,000.00 – This is the exact amount that Connye and Judlyne will receive

If you agree to sell, kindly complete the attached GWD as soon as possible

I know that you two are not "geographically" situated near one another – so,

Option 1

One suggestion is that either one of you get the "notary" component started and then FedEx etc. the original to the other

So that the latter party can sign and have their signature notarized

Option 2

Each of you complete the Signature + notary process and forward the original to me (without the other parties signature etc.)

Which means I would have the same GWD registered twice with Henderson County

Just let me know what will work for you

Please give me a call, or send an email/text if you have any additional questions

Best Wishes,

Clue: Perhaps enough acreage to build a scale-model replica of the Brynhurst property in 5th Ward Houston – Since a decision was made by the elders to sell the home in order to assist in paying for Aunt Maude's nursing home care (Think backward)

September 20, 2022
Joe Harris Email to Second Lead Attorney SE Texas Firm

Good afternoon Attorney Jones,

The general warranty deeds (with the exception of one) have been signed, notarized and recorded with the Henderson County Clerks.

I will be the only "owner" of the 30.8-acre property in Shalene, Texas.

I just spoke with one of my *first cousins* in Houston, Texas.

She and her sister are in the process of completing the signing, and notarizing of the final general warranty deed.

I sent the GWD in Micro Soft Word format to one of the sisters in Cedar Park, Texas – over two (2) weeks ago

Since then I have experienced a kind of "radio silence" from them

I simply did not know what to make of the lack of communication - e.g. they were not responding to my emails, voice mails etc.

As it turns out – we were all on the same page regarding the "suit to partition."

Please let me know if any additional information is required.

Best Wishes,

Chapter Six

The suit to partition received April 20, 2023 had the force of a torpedo blast to the hull of a warship. The text which follows was structured by a representative from the Southeast Texas law firm.

CAUSE NO. _____

JOSEPH HARRIS	§	**IN THE DISTRICT COURT**
Plaintiff		**OF HENDERSON COUNTY,**
		TEXAS
vs.	§	
ISABELLA DELGADO	§	_____ **JUDICIAL DISTRICT**
Defendent		

PLAINTIFF'S ORIGINAL PETITION

TO THE HONORABLE JUDGE OF THIS COURT:

COME NOW, Plaintiff, JOSEPH HARRIS (herein "Plaintiff"), and files Plaintiff's Original Petition complaining of Defendant, ISABELLA DELGADO (the "Defendant"). In support thereof, Plaintiff respectfully shows the following unto the Court.

I.
DISCOVERY LEVEL

1. Discovery will be conducted under a Level 2 Discovery Control Plan pursuant to Rule 190 of the Texas Rules of Civil Procedure.

II.
TRCP RULE 47 CLAIM

2. Plaintiff further alleges that he is seeking monetary relief of $1,000,000.00 or less and nonmonetary relief pursuant to RULE 47(C)(2) OF THE TEXAS RULES OF CIVIL PROCEDURE.

III.
PARTIES

3. Plaintiff, JOSEPH HARRIS, is a resident of Los Angeles County., California, and is represented by counsel.
4. Defendant, ISABELLA DELGADO, residing in Henderson County, Texas, and who may be served with process at (primary address); (secondary address); or wherever she may be found.

IV.
JURISDICTION AND VENUE

5. Jurisdiction over this lawsuit is proper in Henderson County, Texas because this lawsuit is based on an action for partition,

trespass to try title, suit to quiet title, and declaratory judgment in connection with real property located in Shalene, Henderson County, Texas, and the amount of damages in controversy is within this Court's jurisdictional limits.

6. Venue is proper in Henderson County, Texas pursuant to SECTION 15.011 OF THE TEXAS CIVIL PRACTICE AND REMEDIES CODE BECAUSE THIS IS AN ACTION ARISING OUT OF A DISPUTE REGARDING REAL PROPERTY LOCATED IN ANDERSON COUNTY, TEXAS.

V.
FACTS

7. Plaintiff is the co-owner of real property located in Shalene, Henderson County, Texas, (hereinafter referred to as the "Subject Property") being more particularly described as:
   (four (4) parcel numbers for the 30.8 acres)

8. The basis for the claims made herein are Plaintiff's right to title and control of the Subject Property.

9. Plaintiff acquired the Subject Property through intestacy as well as through various deeds and conveyances.

History of the Subject Property

History of the Subject Property

10. From 1898 to 1986, the Heirs of Rosie Edwards have owned the parcel of real property commonly identified as 56 acres of undivided interest. Rosie Edwards is Joseph Harris's great-grandmother.

11. A review of records from a March 3, 1986 Case (case number) (District Court designation) shows (a) The Harris family sued Tommie Lee Wyatt (now deceased) for trespass, (b) Mr. Wyatt counter claimed adverse possession; however before the case was submitted to the court, a settlement was reached

12. The terms of the settlement were as follows; (a) Mr. Wyatt's

claim of adverse possession was dismissed, (b) the Harris family would have an undivided interest in the 56 acres, and (c) Mr. Wyatt would be awarded (tract number, parcel number), composed of approximately 25.2-acres of land. Tommie Lee Wyatt also owned a 50-acre tract to the west of the Subject Land.

13. Referencing the 1986 Interlocutory Judgment in a letter dated September 4, 1986 Mary A. Daffin (counsel for the Harris family) stated (a) Mr. Deuce Taylor (counsel for Mr. Wyatt) would not agree to the inclusion of language regarding partition, and (b) If the matter remained unresolved, the court would decide on how the property should be partitioned.

14. Ms. Annie Wyatt (widow of Tommy Lee Wyatt) then sold the said 25.2-acres to Cody James.

15. In 2006, Ms. Isabella Delgado purchased a 90-acre tract of land to the east of the Subject land.

16. In 2013 Mr. Cody James wrote several letters to the Harris family. The letters outlined legal steps he planned to initiate in an effort to purchase the remaining 30.8 acres.

17. Subsequently, in 2014 Mr. Cody James sold the 25.2-acres to Ms. Isabella Delgado.

18. At the time of the latter transaction, Ms. Annie Wyatt sold an additional 5-acre strip of land to Ms. Isabella Delgado.

19. The 5-acre strip of land was to the south of the Harris Family's 30.8 acres. So, Ms. Delgado's purchase of the 90-acres of land to the east (2006), 25.2-acres of land to the north (2014), and 5-acres of land to the south (2014) effectively landlocked the Harris Family's property.

20. Upon information and belief, Mr. Harris has learned that Ms. Delgado has entered onto and utilized the Harris property for purposes of hunting and has been collecting payments from third-parties for the use of the Harris' property. Ms. Delgado has not provided rental reimbursement to the Harris family for the unauthorized use of their property.

VI.
CAUSES OF ACTION AND REQUESTS FOR RELIEF

Suit to Quiet Title

21. Plaintiff incorporates the preceding paragraphs by reference as if set forth fully herein.
22. Plaintiff asserts a cause of action against Defendants to quiet title to the Subject Property.
23. A party who seeks to remove a cloud from a title to property must plead and prove (i) an interest in specific property, (ii) that title to the property is affected by a claim by the defendant and, (iii) that defendant's claim, although facially valid, is invalid or unenforceable. *See Sadler v. Duvall*, 815 S.W.2d 285, 293 n.2 (Tex.App – Texarkana 1991, den.); *see also La Fleaur v. Kinard*, 161 S.W.2d 144, 147 (Civ.App. – Beaumont 1942, ref. w.o.m.).
24. Plaintiff is the legal and equitable owner of the Subject Property. The Deeds vesting a portion of the Subject Property in Defendants puts a cloud on Plaintiff's title.
25. Plaintiff is entitled to have the cloud(s) upon its title to the Subject Property removed.

Trespass to Try Title

26. Plaintiff incorporates the preceding paragraphs by reference as if set forth fully herein.
27. Plaintiff asserts a cause of action for trespass to try title against Defendants, pursuant to TEXAS PROPERTY CODE SECTION 22.001 AND TEXAS RULES OF CIVIL PROCEDURE 783 – 809.
28. There is exists a justiciable controversy between Plaintiff and Defendants regarding ownership of the Subject Property.
29. The facts set forth herein show that Plaintiff is the actual legal and equitable owner of the Subject Property, and Plaintiff's title to the Subject Property is superior to Defendants.

30. Plaintiff seeks a judgment confirming title to the Subject Property in Plaintiff. Plaintiff is entitled to have the cloud(s) upon its title to the Subject Property removed.

Unjust Enrichment

31. Plaintiff incorporates the preceding paragraphs by reference as though fully set forth herein.
32. In addition to and/or in the alternative to any other cause of action, Plaintiff seeks to recover damages from Defendant for unjust enrichment.
33. Defendant's improper and unlawful use of Plaintiff's Property was wrongful and unjustly enriched the Defendant.
34. Plaintiffs seek to recover the following damages resulting from Defendants' unjust enrichment:
    a. actual damages;
    b. reasonable and necessary attorney's fees pursuant to SECTION **38.001** OF THE TEXAS CIVIL PRACTICE AND REMEDIES CODE;
    c. pre- and post-judgment interest pursuant to **Sections 302.002 and 304.003 of the Texas Finance Code;** and
    d. court costs.

Declaratory Judgment

35. Plaintiff incorporates the preceding paragraphs as if set forth fully herein.
36. In addition to and/or in the alternative to any other cause of action, Plaintiff seeks a declaratory judgment under SECTION **37** OF THE TEXAS CIVIL PRACTICE AND REMEDIES CODE AGAINST DEFENDANT THAT DECLARES AS FOLLOWS:
    a. Plaintiff is the sole legal and equitable title holder of the Subject Property;
    b. Plaintiff is entitled to his share of monies paid to Defendant for the unauthorized use of Plaintiff's property;

c. Plaintiff is entitled to an easement over Defendant's property;
d. Plaintiff is entitled to an easement by necessity over Defendant's;
e. Plaintiff is entitled to an easement at law;
f. In addition to or in the alternative, Plaintiff is entitled to a partition in kind under accordance **Chapter 23 of the Texas Property Code**; and
g. Defendant is not entitled to possession or use of the Subject Property.

Attorney's Fees

37. Plaintiff was required to retain the services of THE SOUTHEAST TEXAS FIRM TO PROSECUTE THIS LAWSUIT.
38. PLAINTIFF SEEKS TO RECOVER THEIR REASONABLE AND NECESSARY ATTORNEY'S FEES INCURRED IN THE PROSECUTION OF THIS LAWSUIT.
39. PURSUANT TO **SECTION 37.009 OF THE TEXAS CIVIL PRACTICE AND REMEDIES CODE**, PLAINTIFF IS ENTITLED TO RECOVER THEIR REASONABLE AND NECESSARY ATTORNEY'S FEES AND COSTS.
40. IN THE ALTERNATIVE, PLAINTIFF SEEKS TO RECOVER THEIR ATTORNEY'S FEES UNDER PRINCIPLES OF EQUITY.

VII.
CONDITIONS PRECEDENT

41. All conditions precedent have been performed or have occurred as required by **RULE 54 OF THE TEXAS RULES OF CIVIL PROCEDURE**.

VIII.
DESIGNATION OF EXPERTS

42. Plaintiff hereby designate the undersigned attorneys, Attorney Bert Hammond, as his expert to testify as to the reasonable and necessary attorney's fees incurred by Plaintiff in the preparation, discovery, and trial of this lawsuit.

IX.
DEMAND FOR JURY TRIAL

43. Plaintiff demands a trial by jury.

X.
PRAYER

WHEREFORE, PREMISES CONSIDERED, Plaintiff, JOE HARRIS, respectfully request that this Court enter a judgment against Defendant, ISABELLA DELGADO AKA ISABELLA L. DELGADO awarding Plaintiff all requests for relief herein, including non-monetary relief, including but not limited to declaratory relief, as well as reasonable and necessary attorney's fees, court costs, and for such other and further relief, both general and special, at law or in equity, to which Plaintiff, JOSEPH HARRIS may show himself to be justly entitled.

In response to the seven page Plaintiff's Original Petition, legal-council for Ms. Delgado submitted a three page Defendant's Original Answer. I received a copy of the latter document on August 7, 2023. A brief summary of the Defendant's response is shown below.

- The Defendant objects to the Plaintiff's Original Petition due to the nature of the allegations
- The Defendant requests that the court sustain the Original Petition and require Plaintiff to replead with more convincing evidence

More specifically, the Defendant objects to the Plaintiff's Original Petition for the following reasons;

- The Petition fails to appraise the Defendant's maximum amount of damages to be sought
- The Plaintiff does not provide facts which support claims made regarding the collection of money, use of the property, or denied use of property
- The Defendant denies each and every, all and singular, the allegations contained in Plaintiff's pleadings, demands strict

proof thereof, and hereby asserts all defenses to which he is entitled under Rule 92 of the Texas Rules of Civil Procedure
- The Defendant denies that she caused any damages or harm to the Plaintiff or the property referred to in this case
- The Defendant denies that the Plaintiff is entitled to attorney fees for Plaintiff's declaratory relief cause of action
- The Defendant pleads the defense set forth in Texas Civil Practice and Remedies Code Section 18.091, requiring Plaintiff to prove loss of earnings, loss of earning capacity, loss of contributions of a pecuniary nature, or loss of inheritance in the form of a net loss after reduction for income tax payments or unpaid tax liability pursuant to any federal income tax law
- The Defendant denies that she has breached any duty owed to the Plaintiff including, but not limited to, the duty of good faith and fair dealing
- The Defendant will show that she is entitled to an award of her costs and reasonable and necessary attorney fees as are equitable and just for defending against the Plaintiff's cause of action for declaratory relief, Tex. Civ. Prac. & Rem. Code Section 37.009.
- The Defendant may have additional defenses that cannot now be articulated due to the generality of Plaintiff's Petition and because discovery is not yet complete
- The Defendant hereby demands a trial by jury

Upon review of "The Defendant's Original Answer," my thoughts drifted to an interesting play on words once shared with me by the late Walter Albert Pittman, Sr. (Uncle Abbey) *Your honor, I deny the allegations, and I resent the allegator!* The Defendant's Original Answer also brought to mind a famous quote used in Shakespeare's *Hamlet*. It was spoken by Queen Gertrude (Prince Hamlet's mother and Queen of Denmark). *The lady doth protest too much, methinks*

A preview of possible outcomes, once the case had been reviewed by the judge and jury, is as follows; the jury could rule; (1) in favor of the plaintiff and grant the separation as well as the easement, (2) against the plaintiff and deny the separation and easement, (3) that the entire 56 acres of undivided interest was to be sold at the fair market value, and (4) that the deed produced by the late Mr. Wyatt was fraudulent and therefore Ms. Delgado was in possession of land that did not belong to her.

Table 5 titled, *Decision Approach by Sadia Maqsood Category* provides a summary of the clues that were linked to the article titled, *5 Genius Tricks For Problem-Solving From the Famous Sherlock Holmes* (S. Maqsood, May 30, 2021). In some ways the table reminds me of the color by number paintings I once created on rainy days as a pre-teen.

Table 5 – Decision Approach by Sadia Maqsood Category

Clue by Date	EASs	NTFDs	CTDs	IPs	POTLSH	Decision Approach
3/31/19 - Survey Team Response					x	Friendly partition or lawsuit (think backwards)
3/31/19 SE TX firm first of two legal agreements					x	Partition Demand Letter (think backwards); Joe Harris paid a $1,450 + $2,794 retainer (connect the dots)
7/1/19 SE TX law firm teleconference					x	Joe Harris must complete affidavits of heirship (always be a skeptic)
12/1/20 attorney from the city that straddled the regional divide between South & CRL Texas - teleconference			x		x x	Easement rights via Mr. Fontenette (think backwards); then sell the property to regain expenditures (always be a skeptic; connect the dots)
4/28/21 – NE Texas law firm legal agreement			x			Joe Harris paid $2,000 – consultation agreement fee (connect the dots)
9/3/21 – NE Texas law firm teleconference	x		x	x	x	Priorities 1 – 4 (CTDs); buyouts (EI); I.D. + Adverse possession (NTFDs); Easement rights (IPs)
9/27/21 – NE Texas law firm – "surprise" teleconference			x		x	Recommendation - obtain encumbrance reports; (observe but not just with the eye)

Clue by Date	EASs	NTFDs	CTDs	IPs	POTLSH	Decision Approach
10/21/21 - SE Texas law firm = signed second of two legal agreements; Paid $1,465			x			Demand for Agreed Sale or Judicial Partition of Real Property (connect the dots)
10/21/21 – SE Texas law firm – Second Lead Attorney - Teleconference			x			Do it all - "If we can't get the implied easement, we will ask for the alternative which would be the separation" (connect the dots)
11/9/21 – SE Texas law firm email to Joe Harris			x			Demand for Agreed Sale or Judicial Partition of Real Property – Included 11/24/21 agreement response deadline (connect the dots)
8/9/22 SE Texas law firm teleconference			x			Partition litigation opposite cotenants – paid $10,000 (connect the dots)
4/20/23 – SE Texas law firm			x			Plaintiffs Original Petition - Suit to Partition (connect the dots)

EASs = engage all senses; sight, hearing, taste, touch, and smell

NTFDs = notice the finer details, not just the glaringly obvious

CTDs = connect the dots. Connect observation A to observation B to observation C etc.

IPs = identify patterns. What are recurring themes, things keep repeating themselves.

POTLSH = Process of thinking like Sherlock Holmes; think backwards, disengage from the task, always be a skeptic, eliminate inessential, observe – but not just with the eye

The witnesses shown below were called to testify on behalf of the plaintiff.

In the interest of brevity, testimony from only three witnesses is presented.

- John Allen, (attorney based in a city that straddles the regional divide between South and Central Texas)
- Larry Blackmon (co-signer affidavits of heirship)
- Austin Cassidy (potential buyer)
- Ruth Farrington (L.V. Jackson's adopted sister
- Edward Fontenette (Shalene, Texas neighbor)
- Stanley Viltz, Representative, Anderson County Appraisal District
- Judlyne Ann Lilly Gibson (first cousin/former owner)
- Brett Hamilton (attorney, First Title Co. of Shalene, Texas)
- Joe Harris (owner)
- Keith Jones (second lead attorney, Southeast Texas Law Firm)
- Danny (Dan) Wilks (first lead attorney, law firm in Northeast Texas)
- Julius Johnston (second lead attorney, law firm in Northeast Texas)
- Representative, Lone Star State Aerial Photography Company
- Virginia Speed, Southern California-based Private Detective
- Bert Hammond (attorney, expert witness)
- Chuck Mitchell, Shalene, Texas Land Survey Co.
- Ava Nelson, Shalene, Texas-based real estate agent
- Franklin (Frank) Peters (attorney who practiced law near the Florida Panhandle)
- John Payton (first lead attorney, Southeast Texas Law Firm)
- Darilyn L. Pittman Thomas (first cousin/former owner)
- James L. Pittman Jr. (first cousin/former owner)
- Walter A. Pittman Jr. (first cousin)
- Connye Yvette Lilly Turner (first cousin/former owner)

Bailiff: Please rise. The Court of the First Judicial Circuit, Real Property Division, is now in session. The Honorable Judge John Meggs presiding. Please be seated.

Judge: Everyone but the jury may be seated. Mr. Lee Masters (Bailiff), please swear in the jury.

Bailiff: Please raise your right hand. Do you solemnly swear or affirm that you will truly listen to this case and render a true verdict and a fair sentence as to this defendant? (Jury answered "I do")
      You may be seated.

Judge: Members of the jury, your duty over the next few days will be to determine whether the dissolution of tenancy in common via (a) a court ordered division of property by way of partition, or (b) by way of sale, is warranted based only on facts and evidence provided in this case. The prosecution must prove that (a) a court ordered partition or (b) the sale of the property is warranted. Conversely, the defense must prove that their opposition to either outcome is justified. However, if you are not satisfied with the arguments presented by the defendant, then reasonable doubt exists and the defendant will be held liable for their position.
      Mr. Allen, what is today's case?

Bailiff: Your Honor, today's case is Joe Harris versus Isabella Delgado

Judge: Is the prosecution ready?

Prosecuting Attorney: (stand up) Yes, Your Honor. (Be seated).

Judge: Is the defense ready?

Defense Attorney: stand up) Yes, Your Honor. (Be seated).

Opening Statements
(Speak at the podium)

Prosecution Attorney: Your Honor, members of the jury, my name is Attorney Bert Hammond. My co-council Attorney Keith Jones and I are representing Joseph Harris in this case. We intend to prove that for nine years, beginning in 2014 and continuing to 2023, the defendant's actions prompted the filing of three charges by category; (1) Suit to Quiet Title, (2) Trespass to Try Title, and (3) Unjust Enrichment. Furthermore we intend to prove that (1) the declaratory judgment, and (2) the awarding of attorney's fees are valid and that the defendant should be held liable for these charges.

Suit to Quiet Title

Plaintiff was the legal and equitable owner of the Subject Property. The Deeds vesting a portion of the Subject Property in Defendants put a cloud on Plaintiff's title

Trespass to Try Title

Plaintiff seeks a judgment confirming title to the Subject Property in Plaintiff. Plaintiff is entitled to have the cloud(s) upon its title to the Subject Property removed.

Unjust Enrichment

Plaintiff seeks to recover the following damages resulting from Defendants' unjust enrichment: (1) actual damages, (2) reasonable and necessary attorney's feeds pursuant to Section 38.001 of the Texas Civil Practice and Remedies Code, (3) pre- and post-judgment interest pursuant to Sections 302.002 and 304.003 of the Texas Finance Code; and (4) court costs.

Please find Isabella Delgado (defendant) liable for these charges. Thank You

Opening Statements
(Speak at the podium)

Defense Attorney: Your Honor, members of the jury, my name is Bo Ryan "Bo" Maverick and my co-council and I are representing Isabella Delgado in this case.

We intend to prove that for the past nine years, beginning in 2014 and continuing to 2023, my client has done nothing to warrant the following charges; (1) a suit to quiet title, (2) the charge of trespass to try title, and (3) the charge of unjust enrichment. Furthermore we intend to prove that (1) the declaratory judgment, and (2) the awarding of attorney's fees should not have been applied, and that the defendant should not be found liable for these charges.

Please find Ms. Elizabeth Delgado not guilty of these charges. Thank you.

Direct Examination (Prosecution)

Judge: Prosecution, you may call your first witness.

Prosecuting Attorney: Thank you, your Honor. I call to the stand Chuck Mitchell, Shalene, Texas Land Survey Co.

Judge: Will the witness please stand to be sworn in by the bailiff. (Witness stands)

Bailiff: (To the witness) Please raise your right hand. Do you swear to tell the truth, the whole truth, and nothing but the truth?

Witness: I do. (Witness goes to the stand and sits down)

PROSECUTION; DIRECT EXAMINATION QUESTIONS FOR WITNESS #1

Prosecuting Attorney: Please state your name for the court.

Witness: Chuck Mitchell

Prosecuting Attorney: On what date were you first contacted by Joe Harris, my client, to conduct a survey of the 56 acres of undivided interest in Salene, Texas?

Witness: I received a letter in the form of an attached file to an email he sent to me on March 26, 2019

Prosecuting Attorney: On what date did you reply to Mr. Harris?

Witness: I responded to Mr. Harris via email on March 31, 2019

Prosecuting Attorney: Kindly provide a brief summary of your March 31, 2019 email response

Witness: I provided the following response to Mr. Harris;

- I reviewed the information that Mr. Harris provided (including a Platt Map)
- It appears that the Harris family owned a total of 30.8 acres undivided interest in the defined 56 acre tract and Ms. Delgado owns the remaining 25.2-acres of undivided interest in the defined 56 acre tract.
- I was unable to establish where a division line separating the two properties would be without agreement by all parties involved.
- The latter step can be accomplished in two ways (1) One way is for all parties (all of the heirs of the Harris family and Isabella Delgado) to come to an agreement as to how to divide the land which is commonly called a friendly partition.
- The second way is through the filing of a partition suit where the court divides the land because the parties could not come to an agreement.
- I recommended that Mr. Harris contact an attorney who is familiar with real estate law in Texas and discuss this matter with them.

- If all parties were able to reach an agreement and provide me with that information, I in turn would provide Mr. Harris with an estimated cost and time frame to perform the survey.
- In addition, for travel planning purposes I informed Mr. Harris that my team did not work on Saturday.

Prosecuting Attorney: Thank you, Your Honor, no further questions

Judge: The Defense may cross-examine the witness.

DEFENSE: CROSS-EXAMINATION QUESTIONS FOR PROSECUTION WITNESS #1

Defense Attorney: Mr. Mitchell did Mr. Harris provide you with factual evidence that confirmed that Ms. Delgado (my client) had refused a request for a friendly partition?

Witness: The pattern of behavior and the amount of time that elapsed in conducting that behavior appeared to infer that Ms. Delgado was opposed to a friendly partition.

Defense Attorney: What do you mean by pattern of behavior and the amount of time that elapsed in conducting that behavior?

Witness: According to a letter I received from Mr. Harris dated March 26, 2019

- His family used to own [parcel number for 25.2 acres].
- In 1986, the court awarded it to Tommy Lee Wyatt (deceased) who owned 50 acres to our west.
- Ms. Annie Wyatt (deceased) then decided to sell the 25.2 acres to Attorney Cody James.
- Ms. Isabelle Delgado purchased the 25.2 acres from Attorney Cody James in 2014.
- During the 2014 transaction Ms. Delgado also purchased a 5-acre strip to the South of our property

- This pattern of behavior essentially land locked the Harris 30.8 acres on the North, East, and South

Defense Attorney: Thank you, Your Honor, no further questions.

Judge: You may step down.

2nd Prosecution Witness

Judge: Prosecution, you may call your second witness.

Prosecuting Attorney: Thank you, your Honor. I call to the stand Joe Harris

Judge: Will the witness please stand to be sworn in by the bailiff. (Witness stands)

Bailiff: (to the witness) Please raise your right hand. Do you swear to tell the truth, the whole truth. And nothing but the truth?

Me: I do. (Witness goes to the stand and sits down)

PROSECUTION'S DIRECT EXAMINATION QUESTIONS FOR WITNESS #2

Prosecuting Attorney: Please state your name for the court

Me: Joseph Harris

Prosecuting Attorney: Mr. Harris, your efforts on behalf of the Salene, Texas property are to be commended. Kindly summarize for the court how you came to become involved with the property.

Me: A brief summary of how I became involved with the property is as follows;

- In 2013, a first cousin requested assistance in paying Geraldine Pittman Wooten's taxes. I agreed to make the payment.
- In 2013, Cody James, a Shalene, Texas, attorney, threatened to file a lawsuit against the Heirs of Rosie. His goal was to force the family to sell the remaining 30.8 acres to him for $400 an acre.
- The first cousins asked me to locate an attorney who would defend the family against the possible lawsuit.
- The attorney I selected was licensed to practice real estate law in Florida, Oklahoma, and Texas.
- The latter attorney provided the first cousins with a plan to purchase the 25.3 acres the family lost as part of a 1986 interlocutory judgment. The cost of the proposed purchase would be $400 an acre.
- Unfortunately, the first cousins were not in favor of the attorney I selected.
- The first cousins were opposed to the fact that he resided in Florida.
- The first cousins also preferred to sell the Shalene, Texas, land as opposed to buying additional property.
- In addition, the first cousins decided to release me from participating in the Shalene, Texas, process because I did not reside in Texas.
- The first cousins then retained the services of a local attorney from a Northeast Texas city.
- The Northeast Texas attorney did not meet the expectations of my first cousins.
- In 2018, one of my first cousins called me and requested additional assistance in paying Aunt Geri's back taxes. At the time, Aunt Geri was residing in a nursing home. The first cousin expressed concern that my aunt's daughter may have stopped making the annual payments. I contacted the Henderson County Tax Assessor's Office. A representative confirmed that Aunt Geri's taxes were in arrears. I promptly paid the past-due taxes.

- However, this time I informed my first cousins that I planned to structure a general warranty deed, which would allow me to assume the place of Aunt Geri on the county tax rolls.

Prosecuting Attorney: Mr. Harris, kindly summarize for the court the Salene, Texas-related tasks you have completed since you first became in involved.

Me: Primarily due to the learning curve involved, it took several years to complete the majority of the tasks. Tasks completed since 2018 have included:

- Used emails to keep the family up-to-date
- Interacted with several title companies on behalf of the family
- Retained the services of a private detective who performed cross checks by social security number and other tasks associated with verifying family linkages
- Structured the Harris Family Tree on ancestry.com
  - People 1,105; Records 1,759; Media 88
  - This step saved the family approximately $5,000 (the amount that a law firm staff member would have charged to complete the task)
  - The latter fee was quoted by a law firm in the North Texas Region.
- Structured and filed 28 affidavits of heirship
  - This step saved the family approximately $6,250
  - The latter fee was quoted by the First Title Company of Shalene, Texas
- Structured and filed ten general warranty deeds,
- Discussed the easement rights pathway with Mr. Fontenette,
- Retained the services of a law firm in Southeast Texas, followed by a firm in the North Texas Region, and returned to the Southeast Texas law firm.
- Contracted with The Lone Star State Drone Company, who provided 1,450 images in 2D Ortho mosaic, and

- Established a Pittman Family Fund Account.
  - The voluntary proceeds were to be used for future activities associated with the Shalene, Texas, property

Prosecuting Attorney: Mr. Harris the various efforts you have described more than likely were time consuming and costly. Kindly share with the court the approximate amount you have expended on Salene, Texas-related activities.

Me: During the period 2013 to present I have spent approximately $42,000 on various Salene, Texas-related efforts.

Prosecuting Attorney: Mr. Harris upon request, did you provide legal counsel with your personal income tax records?

Me: Yes, I provided ten years of personal income tax filings along with one year of corporate filings. I recently requested and was approved for corporate status in the State of California.

Prosecuting Attorney: Mr. Harris, back in 2013 if Ms. Delgado (the Defendant) had agreed to (1) a friendly partition as well as (2) an easement pathway to the county road, across the 5 acre strip to the south, approximately how much would that have cost you?

Me: I estimate the fee to amend Ms. Delgado's deed to allow for an easement path could have been as low as $2,000. I suspect that I would have been charged anywhere from $3,500 to $9,000 by a Salene, Texas survey team for the partition.

Prosecuting Attorney: Mr. Harris can you provide factual evidence that confirmed that Ms. Delgado (the defendant) had refused a request for a friendly partition?

Me: During my initial conversations with Ms. Delgado, my marching orders from the first cousins responsible for paying taxes, were to sell the property. Those orders did not include obtaining the easement rights to the property. However, I believe there is circumstantial evidence that infers that, even if asked, Ms. Delgado had no intention of granting a request for a friendly partition.

Prosecuting Attorney: And what is that evidence?

Me: On April 19, 2018 I received a telephone call from Ms. Delgado. The call was in response to a Certified Letter dated March 19, 2018 that I sent to her as well as a message I left on her landline.

I asked several questions during the April 19, 2018 teleconference including the following;

"Ms. Delgado, how much did you pay for my family's 25.3 acres?"

"Well, I don't rightly recollect, are the taxes current on your 30.8 acres?" she answered.

"Yes, the taxes are current. Ms. Delgado, you wouldn't like it if you had to ask for someone's permission to visit your property," I continued.

" No, I would not," she replied.

"Ms. Delgado, is there a road leading to our property that stretches across the 5-acre strip to the south?"

"Yes, there is a road."

Defense Attorney: Objection, your Honor, the Prosecution has not entered into evidence a transcript of the April 19, 2018 teleconference.

Judge: Sustained, the jury may disregard the witness comments related to the April 19, 2018 teleconference with Ms. Delgado. And those comments will be removed from the record.

Prosecuting Attorney: Do you have any other examples?

Me: Yes, on April 20, 2018 I received an email from Ms. Delgado. In that email she thanked me for reaching out to her and indicated that at this time she had no interest in purchasing the property at the price points I had suggested.

Prosecuting Attorney: What was your response to the latter email?

Me: On April 20, 2018 I sent the following email to Ms. Delgado;
Good afternoon, Ms. Delgado, just a note to confirm receipt of your email. Yesterday, during the teleconference, you initiated you asked me to send you the four (4) closed values for comparable sales in 2016—And I complied with your request. You also asked me to provide you with the source of my confirmed sales information—I complied with your request. As I had to depart for a dental appointment, it was my understanding that you were going to call me today for a follow-up teleconference. It was also my understanding that, during the follow-up teleconference, you were going to provide the price point that you were willing to offer. A major point of disagreement in yesterday's brief teleconference was that—from your perspective our property was landlocked—and the expressed values should be those for landlocked properties. However, from my perspective, you have access to our property from the North, East, and South. This means that for an outside bidder, the property is indeed landlocked—However, for you, it is not landlocked. It is my understanding that our property became landlocked as a result of two (2) simultaneous purchases that you made in 2014. One of those purchases was for our family's former 25.2 acres (to the north), the other for a five-acre strip to the south. You already own the 90 acres that border our property on the east. Instead, of providing me with the expected counteroffer, it appears that you have elected to completely withdraw your expressed decision to purchase the property. Have I correctly interpreted the email correspondence that you sent today?

Prosecuting Attorney: Your honor I move that the email dated April 20, 2018 be admitted into evidence.

Judge: Motion granted. Bailiff you may enter the email dated April 20, 2018 from Mr. Harris to Ms. Delgado into evidence.

Prosecuting Attorney: Mr. Harris is there anything further you wish to add regarding whether or not a request for easement rights was made?

Me: Yes. On May 29, 2018 I sent an email to my first cousins (and family members) In the email I stated "We will need legal assistance to force an easement because Ms. Delgado has refused to voluntarily grant one.

> Good evening [name of first cousin], if legal fees emerged it was definitely my understanding that I had permission to pay those fees, and that I would be reimbursed for those expenditures once the property sold
>
> The *Family View Summaries of Shalene Activities* (*FVSOSAs*) notes were structured to help clarify the latter issues as well as quite a few other issues
>
> However now that you have clearly stated your position regarding legal fees etc. – it appears that Breana Waraksa's offer is the only logical way out.
>
> A review of the *FVSOSAs* notes reveals quite a bit of information....for example,
>
> No one (other than the people who border us on the North, East, South, or West) will be willing to buy this property without an easement
>
> We will need legal assistance to force an easement because Ms. Delgado has refused to voluntarily grant one
>
> After an easement has been granted, we will have to pay a survey team to draw a clear boundary between Ms. Delgado's property and our property
>
> After an easement has been granted, we will have to pay that same (or another) survey team to map out the route for a road – probably on the southern border

This is because Ms. Delgado will probably oppose a request to use her existing road that runs through the 5-acre strip on the South.

At some point we will have to pay a fencing crew to seal off and "gate" the property

Ms. Waraksa called on Saturday – and we had a preliminary conversation –

I have not called her back – because I needed to share the information provided by Ms. Waraksa with the family and obtain feedback/guidance from everyone who wishes to weigh in

I also needed to double-check some facts regarding Ms. Waraksa with the Henderson County Assessment District

Once again, if the family does not want to pool our money and fight for this property, then Ms. Waraksa appears to be the best option

It also appears that Ms. Delgado has elected to ignore my follow-up email request

In that request, I asked her to consider increasing the per acre amount of her original offer of $400 per acre to purchase.
- Best Wishes,

Prosecuting Attorney: Your honor I move that the email dated May 29, 2018 be admitted into evidence.

Judge: Motion granted. Bailiff you may enter the email dated May 29, 2018 from Mr. Harris to Harris family-member into evidence.

Prosecuting Attorney: Mr. Harris is there anything further you wish to add regarding whether or not a request for easement rights was made?

Me: Yes. A review of my notes shows that my last email communication with Ms. Delgado occurred on May 9, 2018. After May 9, 2018, I signed the following legal agreements;

- 3/31/19 Southeast Texas firm - first of two legal agreements
- 4/28/21 Northeast Texas firm legal Agreement
- 10/21/21 Southeast Texas firm - second of two legal agreements

It is my understanding that once those agreements were signed, any further discussion related to easement rights would occur between the firms and Ms. Delgado and/or her legal representative.

I was also informed that each time one of my legal representatives would contact

Ms. Delgado, she would either not return the call or refer them to her legal counsel.

I was also informed that her legal counsel's schedule made it difficult to pin down a firm date to conduct discussions on topics such as easement rights and partition.

In one instance Ms. Delgado's attorney referred my attorney to Brett Hamilton (First Title Co. of Shalene, Texas). Shortly thereafter legal-council informed me that forward progress on discussions related to easement rights, and partitions could not take place until the affidavit of heirship process had been completed.

Prosecuting Attorney: Mr. Harris Have you read the 1986 Interlocutory Judgement?

Me: Yes I have

Prosecuting Attorney: Your Honor, I move to place the 1986 Interlocutory Judgment into evidence.

Defense Attorney: Objection, your Honor. Leading the witness. I fail to see the relevance of the 38 year old court ruling.

Prosecuting Attorney: Your Honor, I have reason to believe that a break in the chain of title to the 25.3 acres occurred as a result of the 1986 Interlocutory Judgment

Judge: Objection over ruled. Bailiff, you may place the 1986 Interlocutory Judgment into evidence.

Prosecuting Attorney: Thank you your Honor. Mr. Harris, do you have any concerns regarding the Judgment?

Me: Yes I do

Prosecuting Attorney: Would you briefly identify for the court the major concerns you have regarding the 1986 Interlocutory Judgment.

Me: I was concerned when I read a letter dated May 10, 1982 from an attorney representing the Pittman family. According to the Harris Family Tree that I structured on ancestry.com, Lee Jackson (following the death of my grandaunt Mattie Edwards Jackson) married Ludie Dials Jackson (deceased). Lee Jackson and Ludie Jackson had three children, Geran Revenell (deceased), L.V. Jackson (deceased), and Ruth Farrington (DOB 6/19/30; not deceased).

- When Lee Jackson died his entire interest in the Shalene, Texas property descended to his son, L.V.
- During the 1986 hearings, Tommy Lee Wyatt presented to the court a deed that was signed by Levi Jackson.
- However, L.V.'s mother informed the attorney that (1) his name was not Levi, (2) he had not adopted the name Levi, and (3) he had never been called Levi.
- Based upon this information the attorney believed that the proposed deed (1) was from a person not in the chain of title, or (2) was a pure forgery.

Prosecuting Attorney: Your honor, I would like to introduce the letter from the attorney who represented the Pittman family dated May 10, 1982 into evidence.

Judge: Does the defense have any objections to the motion?

Defense Attorney: No your Honor

Judge: Bailiff you may place the letter dated May 10, 1982 into evidence.

Prosecuting Attorney: Mr. Harris do you have any additional concerns related to the 1986 Interlocutory Judgment?

Me: Yes, I do

Prosecuting Attorney: Would you briefly identify for the court any additional concerns you may have regarding the 1986 Interlocutory Judgment

Me: I would like to read a handwritten note from Geraldine P. Wooten (Aunt Geri) dated May 13, 1982. The letter casts suspicion on the deed introduced during the 1986 proceedings.

Prosecuting Attorney: You may proceed

Me: Hi Family Members,
     We are attaching copies of our latest correspondence from the attorney. The letter to Albert C. Williams is interesting. It's about our old "Uncle Lee." As far as we know he had no children. Someone is trying to prove he did. A.C. Williams is Louise's son (Louise was Dorothea's daughter) – cc: Maude and Jim

Prosecuting Attorney: Your honor I move that the handwritten note dated May 13, 1982 be placed into evidence.

Judge: The motion is sustained, Bailiff you may place the handwritten note into evidence. The Prosecution may proceed with testimony

Prosecuting Attorney: Thank you your Honor. Mr. Harris are there any other concerns you have regarding the 1986 Interlocutory Hearings?

Me: Yes, In a letter to the Pittman family dated March 19, 1986 Maudell Williams (Aunt Maude) stated the following;
"The amount of land involved was 56 acres. We won all of that back but 3 parcels. Those were given to Tommy Lee Wyatt some time ago by Uncle Buddy (Green Edwards). That was my mother's brother. The other was given away by George Martin, Aunt Rebecca's son, and someone named Levi Jackson gave his part also to Tommy Lee Wyatt. So we get all but those 3 shares. After this land is surveyed, we'll know exactly how many acres we'll have proper and clear title to."

Prosecuting Attorney: What was the exact concern that you had with the excerpt you just read?

Me: The phrase "and someone named Levi Jackson," seems to imply that she was not convinced that Levi Jackson was an heir.

Prosecuting Attorney: Do you have any additional concerns?

Me: Yes. When I compared L.V. Jackson's signature on his draft card to the signature on the deed submitted during the 1986 Interlocutory Judgment Hearings, the signatures did not appear to match.

Prosecuting Attorney: Your honor I move that the draft card and the deed introduced during the 1986 hears be introduced into evidence.

Defense Attorney: Objection your Honor, the witness is not a qualified Document Expert

Judge: Would the Prosecution be opposed to a review of the documents by an independent, qualified Document Expert?

Prosecuting Attorney: The Prosecution would not be opposed to a review of the documents by an independent, qualified Document Expert

Judge: The objection by the Defense is over-ruled. Bailiff pending review by a qualified Document Expert, you may place the copies of the draft card as well as the deed into evidence.

Prosecuting Attorney: Do you have any additional concerns?

Me: Yes, the Obituary for L.V. Jackson displays his name as L.V. Jackson and not Levi Jackson

Prosecuting Attorney: Your honor I move that the Obituary for L.V. Jackson be introduced into evidence

Judge: The motion is sustained, Bailiff you may place the Obituary for L.V. Jackson into evidence. The Prosecution may proceed with testimony

Prosecuting Attorney: Thank you, Your Honor, no further questions.

Judge: Owing to the length of the on-going testimony, and the lunch break hour, the proceedings will take a one and a half hour break. Everyone is due back in the courtroom at 1:00 p.m.

Bailiff: Please rise. The Court of the First Judicial Circuit, Land Division, is now in session. The Honorable Judge John Meggs presiding. Please be seated.

DEFENSE; CROSS-EXAMINATION QUESTIONS FOR PROSECUTION WITNESS #2

Judge: The Defense may cross-examine the witness

Defense: Mr. Harris in your sworn testimony you stated, and I quote;

"I signed the following legal agreements;
- 3/31/19 Southeast Texas firm - first of two legal agreements
- 4/28/21 Northeast Texas firm legal Agreement
- 10/21/21 Southeast Texas firm - second of two legal agreements,"

Was there a reason you changed from the Southeast Texas firm to the Northeast Texas firm?

Me: I was concerned that the legal-council, at the time, did not understand that the property was structured in an undivided interest format. That misunderstanding resulted in an inappropriate assumption for the 3/31/19 Partition Demand Letter.

Defense: Exactly what, in your opinion, was the inappropriate assumption for the 3/31/19 Partition Demand Letter?

Me: The assumption for the 3/31/19 Partition Demand Letter was that Ms. Delgado was a trespasser as opposed to her true status of tenant in common.

Defense: Mr. Harris were there any positive outcomes from what you termed an inappropriate assumption for the 3/31/19 Partition Demand Letter?

Me: Yes, Ms. Delgado was asked to freeze all financial records. And even though the Certified Mail was returned, the firm had a policy of sending a copy of the document via regular mail. So it is safe to assume that she did receive the 3/31/19 Partition Demand Letter. In addition, I was informed by legal-council that the affidavit of heirship process had to be completed before any additional legal action could be taken.

Defense: Mr. Harris, was there a reason you moved on from the Northeast Texas law firm and reestablished contact with the Southeast Texas law firm?

Me: The first lead attorney at the Northeast Texas law firm departed the firm. A second lead attorney at the Northeast Texas firm called and provided additional advice and guidance. That advice and guidance was (1) to sell to Ms. Delgado because even if I was able to obtain a partition my problems with her were not going to end, (2) he didn't like to see his clients spend a lot of money and not obtain the kind of results they were expecting (3) obtain encumbrance reports, and (4) his firm considered my case to be closed.

Defense: Mr. Harris what concern did you have regarding the advice you received to sell to Ms. Delgado?

Me: Ms. Delgado initially offered $400 an acre. She later doubled the offer to $800 an acre. Past actions by Ms. Delgado have resulted in land locking the property. Of course Ms. Delgado has access to the property on three of four fronts. My concern was that comparable properties in the area, that are not land locked and have easement rights are valued at over $2,000 an acre.

Defense: Mr. Harris the Demand for Agreed Sale or Judicial Partition of Real Property dated November 9, 2021 contained a response deadline of November 24, 2021. Kindly explain why this matter is just being heard in March 2024.

Me: I believe the goal was to show the court that we did try to work out a deal. However an agreement could not be reached with Ms. Delgado. I understood that at some point the court was going to want to know, did you try to work this out? Or did you just go straight to the filing of the suit? The Prosecution is now saying to the court, "Well your honor, we did try to work it out, but an agreement could not be reached…So that is when we filed the suit."

Defense: Mr. Harris it is my understanding that you retained the services of a drone operating company. It is also my understanding that images from that service as well as photos taken from your 2019 visit to the property have already been entered into evidence. Do you believe that the drone images your legal counsel has entered into evidence are credible?

Me: Very credible. Each individual photo is geotagged. In the meta data it contains the latitude and longitude of where the photo was taken. These coordinates can be used to locate where the photo was taken. In my opinion, those photos were taken of locations that are within the 30.8 boundaries of the Shalene, Texas property.

Defense; Thank you, your Honor, no further questions.

Judge: you may step down.

3rd Prosecution Witness

Judge: Prosecution you may call your next witness

Prosecuting Attorney: Thank you, your Honor. I call to the stand Ruth Farrington

Judge; Will the witness please stand to be sworn in by the bailiff. (Witness waives her right hand, and then rolls her wheel chair to the front)

Bailiff: (to the witness) Please raise your right hand. Do you swear to tell the truth, the whole truth, and nothing but the truth?

Witness: I do.

Prosecution: Ms. Farrington, Mr. Harris has structured the Harris Family Tree on ancestry.com. Where might you appear in the Harris Family Tree?

Witness: Rosie Burse Edwards, married Hector (H.R., Heck) Edwards. They had eight children. Mattie Edwards Jackson was one of those children. Lee Jackson (Mattie Edwards Jackson) married Ludie Dials Jackson (deceased). Lee Jackson and Ludie Jackson had three children, Geran Revenell (deceased), L.V. Jackson (deceased), and me. I was adopted.

Prosecution: Ms. Farrington, when Lee Jackson died his entire interest in the Shalene, Texas property descended to his son, L.V. During the 1986 hearings, Tommy Lee Wyatt presented to the court a deed that was signed by Levi Jackson. Have you ever referred to your brother L.V. as Levi?

Witness: His name was not Levi. He had not adopted the name Levi. To the best of my recollection, he had never been called Levi.

Prosecuting Attorney: Thank you, Your Honor, no further questions.

Judge: The Defense may cross-examine the witness.

DEFENSE CROSS-EXAMINATION QUESTIONS FOR PROSECUTION WITNESS # 3

Defense: Ms. Farrington, what is your date of birth?

Witness: June 19, 1930.

Defense: That would make you approximately 93 years old

Witness: Women never tell, and I want you to know that I am in possession of all my faculties.

Defense: Over time we all forget small details, is it possible that you could be mistaken about the L.V. versus Levi names?

Witness: No sir, I was present for L.V.'s funeral, and even the obituary that I keep in my Bible refer to him as L.V. and not Levi.

Defense: Thank you, Your Honor, no further questions

Judge: You may step down

A summary of the remaining steps in the Shalene, Texas courtroom process is shown below;
Direct Examination Defense
Defense: Direct Examination Questions for Witness #1
Prosecution: Cross-Examination Questions for Defense Witness #1
2nd Defense Witness
Defense Direct Examination Questions for Witness #2
Prosecution: Cross-Examination Questions for Defense Witness #2
3rd Defense Witness (Defendant)
Defense: Direct Examination Questions for Witness #3
Prosecution: Cross-Examination Questions for Defense Witness #3

Closing Arguments

Judge: Both the prosecution and the defense have now rested their cases. The attorneys will now present their final arguments. Prosecution you may begin.

Prosecuting Attorney: Thank you, your Honor. Members of the jury, over the past few days you have heard testimony about a law suit titled, "The Demand for Agreed Sale or Judicial Partition of Real Property in Salene, Texas."

I would like to remind you of some important information that you should consider in your decision. These facts include;

Beginning in 2013 (when his first cousins asked for assistance) and continuing in 2018 to 2023 Mr. Harris, my client, has taken extraordinary steps to safeguard and secure the family legacy of 56 acres of undivided interest.

The property has been in the Harris family since August 2, 1898

In 1986, the Pittman family sued Tommy Lee Wyatt for trespassing on the Shalene, Texas property.

As a defense, Mr. Wyatt asserted a claim of adverse possession, which the court denied. Adverse possession refers to circumstances under which one may lawfully lay claim to ownership of property not originally one's own.

Wyatt then provided the court with a deed. The signed, notarized deed stated that two "heirs of Rosie," as well as someone Mr. Wyatt claimed was also an "heir of Rosie," had sold the land to him.

It has been demonstrated during these proceedings that the deed introduced by Mr. Wyatt was fraudulent

Rosie Edwards, Mr. Harris' great grandmother, had eight children.

Mr. Harris was able to acquire sole ownership of the remaining 30.8 acres by contacting and subsequently transferring interest from their descendants

Mr. Harris then, retained the services of the Lone Star State Drone Co. who provided 1,450 images in 2D ortho mosaic

The latter images, when combined with several photos taken by Mr. Harris during a 2019 site visit provide credible evidence that Ms. Delgado has been leasing out the Harris portion of the land for at least the past nine (9) years

A neighbor whose property is adjacent to the Harris property has testified that he leases out his land to the deer hunters for $5,000 a year. So, $5,000/year times 9 years (length of time Ms. Delgado has owned land in the area) = $45,000. So the minimum amount owed to Mr. Harris by Ms. Delgado is $45,000

In addition to the easement rights via the shorter route from the County Road, a neighbor who owns a cow pasture to the north is willing to grant an easement via a much longer route.

Suit to Quiet Title

Plaintiff was the legal and equitable owner of the Subject Property. The Deeds vesting a portion of the Subject Property in Defendants put a cloud on Plaintiff's title

Trespass to Try Title

Plaintiff seeks a judgment confirming title to the Subject Property in Plaintiff. Plaintiff is entitled to have the cloud(s) upon its title to the Subject Property removed.

Unjust Enrichment

Plaintiff seeks to recover the following damages resulting from Defendants' unjust enrichment: (1) actual damages, (2) reasonable and necessary attorney's feeds pursuant to Section 38.001 of the Texas Civil Practice and Remedies Code, (3) pre- and post-judgment interest pursuant to Sections 302.002 and 304.003 of the Texas Finance Code; and (4) court costs.

Please find Isabella Delgado (defendant) liable for these charges. Thank You

Judge: Defense you may proceed with your closing argument.

Defense Attorney: Thank you your Honor. Members of the jury, for the past few days you have heard testimony about, "a law suit titled, "The Demand for Agreed Sale or Judicial Partition of Real Property in Salene, Texas."

I would like to remind you of some important information that you should consider in your decision. These facts include;

In 2014 Ms. Delgado acquired her share of the 56 acres of undivided interest by way of an earnest money transaction

At his request Ms. Delgado offered Mr. Harris $800 an acres. This translates into a reasonable and fair per acre dollar amount, given the fact that the property is land locked and does not have easement rights

If the deed introduced in 1986 by the late Mr. Wyatt was fraudulent, it should have been challenged by Mr. Harris' late uncle and aunt. Instead they eventually concurred with the Jackson transaction. This is evidenced by the fact that the name Levi Jackson is displayed on the final page of the 1986 Interlocutory Judgment.

The defense takes issue with Mr. Harris' claim that he is the sole heir of the 30.8 acres property. It is the Defense's position that several missing heirs are still unaccounted for.

The Defense takes issue with the 1,450 images provided by the Lone Star State Drone Co. The majority of those images appear to have been taken of Ms. Delgado's property.

The Defense takes issue with the $45,000 payment due for the alleged use of Mr. Harris' land. The Prosecution failed to demonstrate that Ms. Delgado was leasing out the Harris family property each and every year of the fourteen years (approximately) of her ownership period.

The Defense will not contest Mr. Harris' use of a common road that commences at the end of the 30 acre cow pasture. However, the Defense is opposed to a forced pathway across Ms. Delgado's 5 acre strip to the South.

In reference to the charge of Suit to Quiet Title evidence presented did not show that the Plaintiff was the legal and equitable owner of the Subject Property. Therefore, the deeds vesting a portion of the Subject Property in Defendants does not put a cloud on Plaintiff's title

In reference to the charge of trespass to try title evidence has not been presented that (1) shows that the Plaintiff sought a judgment confirming title to the Subject Property in Plaintiff, and (2) Plaintiff is entitled to have the cloud(s) upon its title to the Subject Property removed.

In reference to the charge of unjust enrichment evidence has not been presented which shows that the Plaintiff sought to recover the following damages resulting from Defendants' alleged unjust enrichment: (1) actual damages, (2) reasonable and necessary attorney's feeds pursuant to Section 38.001 of the Texas Civil Practice and Remedies Code, (3) pre- and post-judgment interest pursuant to Sections 302.002 and 304.003 of the Texas Finance Code; and (4) court costs.

Please find the defendant, Ms. Isabelle Delgado not liable for these charges. Thank You

Jury Instructions

Judge: Members of the jury, you have heard all of the testimony concerning this case. It is now up to you to determine the facts. You and you alone, are the judges of the fact. Once you decide what facts the evidence proves, you must then apply The Law as I give it to you to the facts as you find them.

The Law

Partition of Texas Property, When Joint Owners Cannot Agree by David J. Willis J.D., L.L.M. (https://lonestarlandlaw.com/partition-of-texas-property/)

"Texas law will not force a reluctant joint owner of real property to maintain co-ownership with other persons if he or she does not want to – for any reason. This is part of a broad Texas tradition that no one should be forced to be or remain in business (or jointly-held land ownership) with anyone when they do not want to do so.

The right to a partition is absolute so long as the petitioning party is a joint owner of an interest in the land to be partitioned and has an equal right to possess it along with the other joint owners, subject to any leases. Even the owner of a life estate may compel a partition. Tex. Prop. Code Sec. 23.001. "[Any] joint owner of real property may compel a partition of the interest of the property among the joint owners under Chapter 23 of the Property Code [and Rule 756 et seq. of] the Texas Rules of Civil Procedure." *Wood v. Wiggins*, 650 S.W.3d 533 (Tex.App.—Houston [1st Dist.] 2021, pet. denied).

There is no effective defense to a partition action that is properly brought by someone who qualifies. *Spires v. Hoover*, 466 S.W. 2d 344 (Tex.App.—El Paso 1971, writ ref'd n.r.e.).

There are two potential pathways in seeking a partition: "Partitions may be in kind (meaning that property is divided into separate parcels and each parcel is allotted to a separate owner) or by sale (meaning that property is sold and sale proceeds are divided among the owners)." *Bowman v. Stephens,* 569 S.W.3d 210 (Tex.App.—Houston [1st District] 2018, no pet.).

Property Code Chapters 23, 23A, and 29, as well as Rules 756-771 of the Rules of Civil Procedure apply to partition actions. Section 23.001 states:

A joint owner or claimant of real property or an interest in real property or a joint owner of personal property may compel a partition of the interest or the property among the joint owners or claimants under this chapter and the Texas Rules of Civil Procedure.

The owner of a non-possessory interest can neither seek nor oppose a partition action. *Dierschke v. Cent. Nat'l Branch of First Nat'l Bank*, 876 S.W.2d 377 (Tex.App.—Austin 1994, no writ).

Partition is by definition a dissolution of joint ownership (tenancy in common). "An undivided possessory interest in property is a tenancy in common. . . . Partition dissolves a tenancy in common, vesting in each owner a sole estate in a specific portion of land. . . . Partition of a tenancy in common affects the right to possession, but not the title of the property. . . . Partition [in kind] leaves title as it was, but segregates the rights of owners, locating them in distinct parts of the premises. . . . Partition thus enables cotenants to sever their rights of possession [away from the whole] and thereafter hold exclusive possession of specific parts of property to which all joint owners [previously] had an equal right of possession prior to partition." See *Dierschke*, cited above.

The right to partition may be waived or contracted away by agreement of the parties. If an agreement among the parties to divide the property is reached, a party who later decides to pursue a legal partition action will be estopped from asserting such a right, so long as the other parties affirmatively plead the defense of waiver and estoppel. See *Wood*, cited above.

Since personal as well real property is mentioned in Property Code Section 23.001, the right to partition extends not just to the realty but also the personal property (furniture, fixtures, and equipment) that may be located on the premises.

No statute of limitations applies to the right of partition. *Pate v. Ballard*, 634 S.W.3d 957 (Tex.App.—Waco, 2021, no pet.).

Judge: In just a moment, the bailiff will take you to the jury room to consider your Verdict. One of the first things you will want to do is to select a foreperson. It will be the foreperson's duty to sign the verdict form when you have agreed on a verdict. Whatever verdict you render must be unanimous which means that each and every person must agree on the same verdict. The Bailiff will now escort you to the deliberation room.

Bailiff: All Rise. (Stand, get verdict form from the judge and escort Jury to deliberation room)

Judge: (When the Jury Returns) Have you reached a verdict?

Jury Foreperson: We have, your Honor.

Judge: What say you?

Jury Foreperson: We the jury, in the case of Joseph Harris versus Isabella Delgado, find the defendant (guilty/not guilty) of the charge(s) of.......................

Judge: (After verdict is read) Thank you, Jury, for your service the past few days. Court is adjourned.

March 8, 2024:
Joe Harris Letter to Family and Friends Regarding the Shalene, Texas, Property

On Monday, March 4, 2023, I went to Shalene, Texas where two attorneys from a Southeast Texas law firm represented me in the suit to partition. They were great! I flew in from LAX early Monday morning with the intention of being in court just a few days. Several parties also made the sojourn to Shalene, Texas including Wally (*first cousin*), Jimmy (*first cousin*) and Larry (a close friend of the family). Collectively the group transformed into a cohesive support team. The encouragement, warmth and understanding they brought to the judicial setting was invaluable. Wally, Larry, Jimmy and I ended up having to spend two nights and being in court three days.

After hearing both sides, Joseph Harris vs. Isabella Delgado, the judge agreed that the property should be partitioned in accordance with the 1986 Interlocutory Judgment. However, there was a surprising twist to the story. The judge awarded me an additional 9.2 acres. This was because a handwriting expert noted a discrepancy between Levi Jackson's signature on the deed introduced in 1986, and L.V. Jackson's signature on his draft card. The ruling increased my total ownership in Shalene, Texas property to 40 acres. The judge also agreed to the proposed easement route that ran along the outer edge of a 32.9-acre cow pasture to the north and continued along a private road (the long way). In addition, a second easement was granted that began at the county road to the south and continued across the 5-acre strip owned by Ms. Delgado (the short way). I answered questions on the stand to the best of my ability and also entered into evidence encumbrance reports, affidavits of heirship and general warranty deeds. The documents supported the position that I was the sole owner of the property.

The amount of land involved in the 1986 Interlocutory Judgment was 56 acres. In 1986, the Pittman family won all of that back but 3 parcels. Those were given to Tommy Lee Wyatt some time ago by Green Edwards. That was my grand uncle. The other was given away by George Martin, my *first cousin* once removed, and someone named Levi Jackson gave his part also to Tommy Lee Wyatt. So the Pittman family got all but those 3 shares. Once again, I now have proper and clear title to 40 of the original 56 acres.

Essentially the judge ruled that I have the legal right to the peaceful enjoyment of the property. However he did caution that failure to monitor and manage the land can invite neighbors and others to develop a strong case for seeking ownership via adverse possession. Adverse possession allows a trespasser to become the owner of land they do not own if they meet certain criteria and bring an action in court asking a judge to declare them the owner. To avoid this possibility, "no trespassing" signs should be posted. In addition, if a family member or friend is unable to check the land periodically, a manager should be hired. The judge decided to refer all issues linked to financial matters to mediation. So, the final determination on topics such as (a) whether I should be reimbursed for the several years Ms. Delgado has been leasing our portion of the property to deer hunters as well as (b) reimbursement for legal services will be issued at a later date.

The most important issue facing me now is budgeting for projected costs. To date, I have spent approximately $46,000 on various legal fees including the suit to partition as well as the buy-out amounts for four family members. Several family members have contributed $2,400 to a Pittman Family Fund. The Fund was set up to assist in addressing future Shalene, Texas – related costs. Examples of anticipated expenditures as well as projected estimates for Mandatory (M) , Essential (E), Desirable (D) Ratings include;

M - fee for the survey team $3,500 (This is an average value – It is possible the survey could cost more.)

M – A southeast Texas law firm fee to amend Mr. Fontenette's (friendly neighbor to the north) and Ms. Delgado's deeds for the easement rights $2,000. (The dollar value for the easement strips still needs to be negotiated.)

M – barbed wire fencing to separate the 32.9 acres from Ms. Delgado's 25.8 - acres
$1,715 (estimated value that could be more or could be less)

M – prefabricated pedestrian bridge over a 7-foot-wide (approximately) stream
$2,778 (cost of the preferred bridge – there are lesser priced bridges)

M – Annual property taxes $994.64 (approximately) –
Grand total for Projected Mandatory Estimates = $10.987.64 (approximately)

E – fencing to protect Mr. Fontenette's cows (To Be Determined, TBD)

E - a possible gravel road (TBD)

E - brush and dead trees clearance (TBD)

E - cost of a "property sitter" to walk through the grounds on a regular basis, relay updates, send photos, and possibly supervise various repairs (TBD)

E – strategically placed remote cameras (TBD)

E- porta potty rentals as well as a trash pick-up service (TBD)

E – Installation of a sewer line

E – The easement rights for gas, water, and electrical lines (TBD)

A primary motivating factor for assuming sole ownership of the property was to ensure that the 30.8 acres (now 40 acres) remained in the family. The original 56 acres had been in the family since 1898. Prior to the transfer of interest, a group of five *first cousins* did their best in terms of keeping the taxes current and reaching a consensus on issues such as sale versus partition. Since assuming sole ownership, I am now fully responsible for payment of all projected expenditures. However, several family members have expressed a desire to visit the property for the purpose of conducting activities such as family reunions, camping, and picnics.

A Pittman Family Fund was established to complement and supplement expenditures for various projected costs. Voluntary contributions will be welcomed. In addition to on-going expenditures, the proceeds may be used to pay the annual tax bill.

As usual, checks or money orders can be made payable to Joe Harris. I will then deposit the funds into the Pittman Family account.

I trust this letter has not been too long, but wanted you to know about these exciting and yet challenging developments. Please give me a call or send me an email if you have any additional questions. Thank you

The Shalene, Texas court proceedings began on March 4, 2024 and ended Two days later on March 6, 2024. A total of eleven years had gone by since my 2013 invitation to join the *first cousins* in the Shalene, Texas scenario. Adherence to annual income tax requirements prompted me to keep track of all Shalene, Texas expenditures. So far, those expenditures (including $14,000 in buy-outs as well as $10,000 for the suit to partition) have reached the $46,000 mark. To place the latter value in proper context, the family had once considered (1) selling all 30.8 acres to Isabella Delgado for $24,640 (minus approximately $6,250 in affidavit of heirship fees), or (2) Austin Cassidy, who proposed a $33,880 options agreement.

In reference to the $46,000 plus value, Lena Horne, an American dancer, actress, singer, and civil rights activist, is often credited with saying, "It's not the load that breaks you down... it's the way you carry it." The quote has also been attributed to Lou Holtz (American former football player, coach and analyst) and C.S. Lewis (a British writer and Anglican lay theologian). It is unclear as to who actually said it first. Although I never had a conversation with Lena Horne, my mother, Florence Harris, did. In 1968 my family moved to a home on 9th Avenue on the west side of Los Angeles, and she was one of our neighbors.

Reflecting back on my 2019 visit, I knew that the Shalene, Texas, property could easily become a favorite go-to getaway destination for peace and tranquility. Traversing the densely wooded terrain could provide a boost to the cardio element of my daily exercise routine. It could also present a form of meditative relaxation through total emersion in a pine tree–laden wilderness. It was an environment that was totally different from the fast-paced streets and highways of Southern California. I envisioned that in the springtime, colorful patches of azaleas would be sprinkled throughout the lush green canopies of towering trees. Each of the specialized flora and native fauna underscoring the pristine landscape's historic significance and rare natural beauty.

I recalled thinking, *How truly peaceful it must be throughout the changing of the seasons. Here in this setting, where 100 foot tall pines ascend to greet azure blue skies. A place where radiating sun showers illuminate dew laden leaves and caress the rugged landscape.* I also envisioned that *a*s I navigated the late March to mid-May brush and vegetation, shadows from the overhanging trees would dance playfully across my red clay covered boots. Shadows in the form of dark colorless patterns that ebbed and flowed as if choreographed by a wind, rustling through skyward-reaching pink and white dogwood tree roots.

On Thursday March 7, 2024, the day after the conclusion of the Shalene, Texas, hearings, several parties joined me for a walk-through of the property. A small herd of about 15 cows were waiting for us at Mr. Fontenette's 32.9-acre spread just north of the property. The bovine began to move toward us from all four corners of the fenced-in property. Each of the Holsteins appeared to be at least 4 feet, 10 inches tall at the shoulder. As previously noted, prior to 2019, the last time I was that up close and personal with large bovines was during my preteen summer visits to Mama Lilly's Farm in Hempstead, Texas.

I repeated a phrase I first uttered in 2019: "Looks like we got ourselves a welcoming committee!"

Mr. Fontenette again replied, "The reason they coming at us like this, is they think they are about to get fed."

Similar to 2019, Mr. Fontenette turned to the truck bed and almost effortlessly, hoisted a 50 pound sack of feed onto his right shoulder. He then proceeded to dump the contents into the feeding trough.

At the conclusion of the feeding, Mr. Fontenette led the way across the pasture to a rear gate and down an uneven dirt road that contained embedded tire tracks. The first stop was a small sized pond.

Repeating another 2019 comment, Mr. Fontenette stated, "I had a problem a few years ago with a beaver who got up in here and was clogging up the pond, but after a while, he went away."

Larry, who resided in the Houston, Texas, area, added, "Over there I think I see signs where wild pigs have been foraging for roots."

Mr. Fontenette replied, "That's right, the good thing about hiking through here this time of year is that the snakes are in hibernation."

Larry then commented, "And that's why I brought a machete, some bear spray and a Glock. Hey! did I ever tell you guys about the time I went hunting with a buddy back in my college days?"

Although I nodded that I was familiar with the story, Larry ignored my affirmation and began to share with the group the up close and personal encounter with a mama pig.

Upon completion of the story, Mr. Fontenette commented, "Now, that's quite a tale you got there!"

As the group of five continued to walk up the inclining dirt road, we encountered the second, much larger-sized pond. The family members took turns taking photos and videos of the babbling pond. The rather large pond was actually situated on the heirs' property. At some point, I surmised, the road surrounding the pond would have to be smoothed out and graded. The landscaping task would be in preparation for the proposed family reunion table-and-chair set up.

The temperature had risen from a low of 38 degrees last night to a high of 62 degrees Fahrenheit today. However, it was still cold enough to prompt that annoying trickle of mucus to ooze from my left nostril.

Much like Austin Cassidy, Jimmy, my first cousin, proved to be a regular Inspector Gadget. Included among the items in Jimmy's backpack were a GoPro Camera, water, and snacks. Based upon my 2019 outing, I knew the large pond was just the beginning of the fascinating sojourn through this legacy of generational wealth.

Similar to my reflections in 2019, about halfway through a heavily wooded area, I began to speculate about the kaleidoscope of pastel-colored changes in foliage that were associated with seasonal transitions.

Pointing to a barbed wire fence, Mr. Fontenette said, "I think right about here is where my property ends and your property begins, so it looks like we need to climb over that fence."

I was quite pleased that Mr. Fontenette used the phrase "your property" when addressing me. The recent court ruling was finally starting to sink in. According to the courts, all 30.8 acres now belonged to me.

Similar to the experience in 2019, I still wasn't prepared to climb over that first barrier - a barbed wire fence. Essentially the group of five were out there in the middle of nowhere – and the process of straddling a barbed wire fence could end poorly. So, it took a little bit of persuasion and a partial tree stump that Jimmy found for me to stand on. The general idea was to push down with my left hand on an un-barbed portion of the fence and combine the spring action torque from the wire with an upward sling of my right leg to get up and over. Similar to 2019, the heavy boots I was wearing simply gave me additional pause for concern.

Owing to the sinewy strength in his long legs, Mr. Fontenette didn't have any problems clearing the barrier. Surprisingly enough, I managed to get my five-foot eleven frame over the fence with no problems. Although not injured, a piece of Jimmy's jacket did come in contact with a barb. After handing me his can of bear spray, Glock and machete, Larry, owing to his earlier years of athletic training, managed to get up and over with no problem. Wally also cleared the barrier with ease and afterward commented, "Man! I can't wait to get my three sons here on a camping trip! Of course, two of them are based in Alaska, so getting all of them here at the same time might be a tall order."

In reference to camping, I spent some time on the internet searching by key word topics such as portable camping toilets and digging a latrine (a flashback to my Boy Scouts days), portable camping showers, and portable handwashing stations. Fortunately, the court ruling also addressed the easement rights for the water, gas, electric and sewer lines. However, in lieu of tapping into a sewer line, I hadn't quite ruled out the installation of a septic tank.

Although hindered by funding concerns, I have strongly considered building permanent structures. Initially I envisioned a park ranger-style cabin mounted at the top of four flights of stairs. The exterior of the cabin would be surrounded by an observation deck with 360 degree views. There would be a screened-in clearing after the second flight of stairs that could be used for outdoor dining or sleeping. It would be designed to blend in like a tree house with the surrounding pine tree forest. The actual cabin would probably be constructed on a supportive iron frame. For security purposes, it was possible to surround the base of the cabin with at least a twelve-foot tall wrought iron fence. The fence would help safeguard the cabin from unwarranted intruders during lengthy periods of absence. To accommodate guests, it might be possible to construct additional cabins.

However, more recently my thoughts have drifted to even more lofty goals. Perhaps a compound complete with a two-story main house and at least one attached guest house. It might be possible to encircle the structure(s) with a combination of wrought iron and stone fencing. I envisioned a paved road leading to a main gate that opened to reveal a semicircular System Pavers–style driveway. The pavers could flow underneath a second-story guest bedroom and extend to a rear parking area. I also remained open to a dwelling that was patterned after several Scandinavian architectural designs. The latter designs could incorporate A frame–style models or two-story, rustic barn–style concepts.

We successfully cleared the barbed wire barrier, only to encounter thick brush and heavy vegetation. Similar to my observations in 2019 there was sleet on the ground and in the trees. The sleet often resembled shards of scattered broken glass.

We then traversed a long, winding dirt trail that was flanked by 100 foot tall pine trees. Larry, armed with his machete, led the way. Throughout the journey, my true preference was to gaze upward at the frosty beauty of the tree-lined horizon. However, the floor of the darkened woods was thick with ropelike vines. And if your foot hooked one of those vines the wrong way, it could easily take you down.

Looking downward was good practice for the spring when the snakes were out and about. Accidently startling or stepping on a poisonous snake could prompt it to bite in self-defense. I researched snake gaiters and snake chaps on the internet and definitely planned to wear protection in the spring. Several of the snake gaiter websites mentioned that most bites will occur between the ankles and the knees. The assumption being that you do not plan to pick up and/or handle the snake. In reference to snakes six feet in length, researchers mentioned a four foot strike range. When venturing into the rugged terrain that Shalene, Texas (or Mother Nature) offers it is a good idea to have snake anti-venom on hand.

As we navigated our way through the dense brush and heavy vegetation, I couldn't help but think, *What if, the vines wrapping around my boots from the floor of the woods were the symbolic hands of my ancestors grouping at my ankles and thanking me for not selling?*

To my surprise we encountered a familiar small patch of yellow daffodils in an open clearing. It was as though the cluster of flowers was an early sign that spring would soon be on the way. Moving past the daffodils, and about halfway through the passage, we encountered a second barrier – a six-foot wide creek. The creek appeared to separate one side of the property from the other.

I used a 50 foot laser tape measure purchased online to gauge the average length of the ravine. A future goal was to place a foot bridge across the divide. I planned to name it the Rosa Edwards Bridge. Similar to the group in 2019, we decided to broad jump across the creek. This time I remembered to pack an extra pair of Levi's just in case I returned to the hotel sporting an extra coat of mud. It just wouldn't do for me to board a return flight to LAX with my pants knees all muddy from the jump. Fortunately I was able to grab the other side of the sloping ravine, without brushing my knees.

As the journey continued, we encountered the several large areas that can best be described as clearings as noted in the 2019 visit. The open areas were natural landing spots for a helicopter. Prior to the 2019 site visit, I had a teleconference with a local helicopter pilot. The strategy was that he would drop me off in one of the clearings and I would hike into the property and meet up with Mr. Fontenette. After the teleconference, Austin Cassidy mentioned that he was opposed to the helicopter drop-off strategy as he was afraid of flying. As previously noted, the latter statement in conjunction with the following voice mail message on my cell phone from the pilot, prompted me to scrap the helicopter option.

The helicopter pilot's voice mail reference to the need for a flat stretch, perhaps 100 foot by 100 foot minimum of clear grass was important for convenient entry and possibly emergency exit from the property. I certainly made a mental note to ensure that a helicopter landing pad was included in future plans should I decide to retain the property.

Addressing me, Jimmy said, "Joe it's really easy to keep your bearings in here," That's when he showed me the Google Maps feature that was downloaded to his cell phone.

From my perspective, without Google Maps and/or a compass, the thick brush, heavy vegetation and meandering trails, could have easily resulted in some degree of disorientation. When researching the question, "How many acres is a full sized football field?" The resulting answer is about 1.32-acres. So, 30.8 acres (the *heirs* share of the former 56 acres) is almost 41 full sized football fields.

It was at this stage of the journey that we observed deer hunting blinds as well as deer feeding stations had been removed, from the clearings. The 2019 photos as well as the 2022 drone images proved to be instrumental in verifying their prior existence. Of course, the white-tailed deer is the species native to the Henderson area.

Probably due to the rather chilly temperature, as well as the amount of hiking, climbing and jumping involved, I suspect Florence, my late mother, would have paused and waved good bye to me at the barbed wire fence. For her that probably would have been a *déjà vu* reminder of the time she watched me climb over a six-foot cinder block wall in pursuit of a burglar. Only this time she wouldn't be horrified by my actions.

As previously noted, similar to her Houston, Texas-based brother Jim, and sisters Maude, Anne and Geraldine, my mother also sang in a choir. Choir rehearsals were held at Neighborhood Community Church in Los Angeles, California. The church was situated about a half block from our home on 48th Street.

Reflecting back on my 2019 visit, I once again closed my eyes and imagined my mother there with me in spirit for part of the journey. Florence Harris was a firm believer in the power of prayer. So I am sure she would have enjoyed listening to traditional songs. On that day, however, I suspect contemporary music might have streamed from her earbuds.

Reflecting upon her many favorites, those songs probably included; Harry Belafonte "Matilda," Sarah Vaughan "Fly Me to the Moon," Billy Eckstine "My Foolish Heart," "The Days of Wine and Roses," Nat King Cole "When Sunny Gets Blue," "Autumn Leaves," The Flamingos, "I Only Have Eyes for You," Nancy Wilson "Who Can I Turn To," "(You Don't Know) How Glad I am," Dionne Warwick "Walk on By," Louis Armstrong, "Summertime with Ella Fitzgerald (from Porgy & Bess)," and "Home" by Stephanie Mills.

Addressing Mr. Fontenette, Jimmy said "Mr. Fontenette, the inclining road we are walking seems to lead straight to the property.

"That's right," Mr. Fontenette answered

Referencing the use of the private road to access the property, Jimmy added,

"In Texas, a person has a right of access over a private road at all times and for all purposes."

That's when Jimmy said

"Mr. Fontenette, thank you for granting Joe the *easement* rights to access the property"

"You're welcome, it was the very least I could do given the circumstances," Mr. Fontenette answered.

Wally then reminded us that he had agreed to return to the L.A. area in time for his daughter's renewal of her wedding vows. Adding that it was probably time for all of us to get back to the hotel. Which was fine with me, because we had re-scheduled our return flight so as to accommodate the drive back to the rental car location.

Similar to 2019, the group decided not return the same way we entered the property. I definitely approved of the latter decision because I wasn't looking forward to a rematch with the barbed wire fence. The alternate route allowed us to walk across one of the fallen 100-foot tall trees. The tree had conveniently come to rest on top of another stretch of barbed wire fencing. I would later reference the second barbed wire fence as the third barrier. Needless to say, the fallen tree provided a welcomed passage for my weary feet and legs.

This time I remembered to avoid a potentially fourth and final barrier upon returning to the cow pasture. The rental car was left on a dryer patch of road just outside of Mr. Fontenette's locked gate. That was because in 2019, owing to the recent rains, the tires had become entrenched in the muddy driveway.

When we returned to the hotel, I took a few minutes to scrape and rinse the thick red clay from the soles of my boots. I then quickly gathered my belongings and checked out of the room. I still hadn't mastered the fine art of programming the navigation feature in my cell phone. Fortunately, both Jimmy and Wally were familiar with the technology and the group was soon on its way back to the Dallas Fort Worth airport.

The mid-afternoon traffic was a little more congested in comparison to the wide open highway we traversed during the middle of the night. The two hour drive back to the rental car location proved uneventful. Prior to the trip to Shalene, Texas, I had been adhering to an almost daily walking routine. As a result, I somehow managed to avoid my 2019 experience with painful leg cramps. Jimmy's training and participation for Los Angeles area *CicLAvia* events definitely assisted his physical conditioning.

In between marveling at the scenic landscape that framed the rustic background along the way, the *voices in my head* began to fade in and out of focus. I remain optimistic that someday the heirs of Rosie will be able to hold a reunion on the grounds of property that has been in the family for the past 126 years. For the past few decades, the heirs of Rosie have collectively mounted efforts on behalf of the property.

In many ways, these efforts seem to mirror the struggles of families referenced in an article titled, "Black Owned Land is Under Siege in the Brazos Valley," N. Blakeslee & J. Heid, *Texas Monthly, News & Politics*, November 2023; https://www.texasmonthly.com/news-politics/heirs-property-black-owned-land-brazos-county/

A summary of the article is shown below;

- Acre by acre families have lost long-held property near Bryan and College Station, Texas
- A great deal of the loss has been due to the efforts of two men who weaponized documents that are known or understood by only a few people, to acquire plots potentially worth millions
- A specific tract of land referenced in the article was termed heirs' property
- Heirs' property is land passed down from generation to generation without the use of wills
- This is not an unusual form of ownership in Black communities
- In general, Black communities are characterized by (a) a lack of access to attorneys and (b) a lack of funds to pay for them
- Much of the acreage held by Black families in Brazos County and throughout the south is heirs' property
- This pattern is a reflection of (a) a legacy of regional poverty and (b) a lack of trust in White attorneys and the court system during the Jim Crow era
- Unique to heirs' property is that it becomes more diffuse as new generations have children
- As a result, any individual heir may own only a tiny percentage of land, known as an "undivided interest."

The three hour fifteen minute one way flight from Dallas Fort Worth to Los Angeles International Airport (LAX) afforded even more time for reflection. Maudell Williams' (Aunt Maude) letter provided the next generation with a chief corner stone to build upon. Clues provided in the letter, when combined, would later serve as an anchor in the midst of a stormy sea. These invaluable clues also highlighted the myriad of problems linked to the property.

The goal of the descendants of Rosie was to chart a strategy to address an on-going problem that had been lingering for decades. Similar to a technique used by fire fighters, some clues served as fire line safety nets. Like pearls of wisdom sprinkled along the way, these clues were passed from generation to generation in writing as well as by word of mouth. However, when it came to implementing a future course of action, not all clues had the same impact. This fact underscored the need to prioritize clues linked to topics such as sell versus partition.

Similarities emerged when comparing the Shalene, Texas dilemma and a jigsaw puzzle approach often employed by crime scene detectives. By definition, a jigsaw puzzle is any set of varied, irregularly shaped pieces. When these pieces were properly assembled, they form a picture or map. In Henderson County, the four parcels of *heirs'* property were displayed in a Henderson County *Platt Map*. The map also included a fifth parcel which represented the 25.3-acres that were relinquished to the encroaching neighbor in 1986. The steps used by detective Sherlock Holmes proved to be of assistance in addressing the Shalene, Texas predicament.

According to Sadia Maqsood (published writer, editor and blogger), "the point of thinking like a detective is to be able to make better judgments, to predict things ahead of time, to come up with practical solutions to everyday problems, and to keep your brain's creative machinery running." (S. Maqsood, 5 Genius Tricks For Problem-Solving From the famous Sherlock Holmes, May 30, 2021). Sadia Maqsood also noted that adherence to the latter steps would enable the researcher to; (a) come up with a testable hypothesis and (b) make predictions instead of jumping to conclusions without evidence. A conclusion could be drawn that these steps make detective work seem almost elementary.

Holmes rebuffed praise that declared his abilities to be *elementary*. In fact, the oft quoted phrase *elementary my dear Watson*, never actually appeared in Conan Doyle's writings. However, Holmes did offer some insight into his method by claiming *when you have excluded the impossible, whatever remains, however improbable, must be the truth*.

According to Francine Miller (November, 2022), historically, when a court ordered partition of heirs' property by sale, the land was sold to the public. This typically happened by a mandatory sale at an auction. Often, property owners lost their family legacies and generally received a small percentage of what the land was worth – far below the property's fair market value. This has resulted in a tremendous amount of land loss among African Americans (disproportionately) and other people of color in the United States.

Benoit Morenne also referenced loss of family legacies in an article titled "A descendant of freed slaves, financier pursues family's $900 million oil claim," (The Wall Street Journal, November 21, 2023). In the article Kneeland Youngblood alleged that his family was deprived of the riches from oil-soaked land and is suing Conoco Phillips. As previously noted, a major company had been slant-drilling oil from the Shalene, Texas property. As a result, royalty checks were sent to my mother and her siblings. My mother was quite upset when the checks stopped coming. Citing declining oil reserve levels, the oil company determined drilling was no longer cost-effective.

The truth associated with the Shalene, Texas property may have been that it was my destiny to be called upon to assist in deciphering clues. Those clues eventually led to the unraveling of a myriad of problems linked to the property. The process enabled me to assist in charting a strategy to address a series of obstacles that had been impeding my family's journey for decades.

I first experienced what the late Robert Pittman (Uncle Bobby), would term a *mitiblende* moment at age five. That moment occurred because I inadvertently failed to heed his warning. Reflecting back on that incident I recall thinking, *Here I am with my five year old derriere hanging out all undignified-like over the Los Angeles River.* Seventy-two years later, I experienced another *mitiblende* moment. This time I took notice of the clues left by my late aunts and uncle. In so doing I avoided using the expression, *Here I am with my seventy-six year old derriere hanging out all undignified-like over the Sanchez River.*

Essentially the 56 acres of undivided interest represented the transfer of generational wealth in the form of heirs' property by Rosie Edwards, my great-grandmother. In reference to the family story linked to the Shaline, Texas property, the following statement definitely applies, *Parents not including estate planning in occasional dinner table discussions could position their children for future legal problems.*

It is true that some of the best goals in life are not easily obtained. However, it is equally true that the Sadia Maqsood approach made the achievement of the Shalene, Texas goals well worth the struggle. I reflected on the renowned literary expression of Douglas Malloch in *Good Timber.*

Good timber does not grow with ease:
The stronger wind, the stronger trees;
The further sky, the greater length;
The more the storm, the more the strength.

Appendixes – Heirs' Property

The following definitions are from multiple sources and are not specific to any particular state statute. Of course, any statutory definitions (terms defined in the laws of a particular state) would overrule these definitions in any legal proceeding.

- Heirs' property (sometimes known as family land) is property that has been transferred to multiple family members by inheritance, usually without a will. Typically, it is created when land is transferred from someone who dies without a will to that person's spouse, children, or other heirs who have a legal right to the property.
- When heirs' property is created, the heirs own all the property together (in legal terms, they own the property as "tenants in common"). In other words, they each own an interest in the undivided land rather than each heir owning an individual lot or piece of the land.
- In addition to the above, unless the heirs go to the appropriate administrative agency or court in their jurisdiction and have the title or deed to the land changed to reflect their ownership, the land will remain in the name of the person who died.
- To resolve heirs' property issues, an important first step is tracing the ownership of the land from the original titled owner to the current owners. Many practitioners encourage heirs' property owners to build a family tree identifying all the heirs, deceased and living.
- When a person dies with a valid will, they die "testate" and their will determines who inherits their property. When a person dies without a will, they die "intestate" and state law governing intestate succession determines who inherits that person's real estate and other assets. Who inherits a person's land by intestate succession varies depending on which family members survive the decedent

- Heirs who inherit land intestate (without a will) own it as tenants in common. Tenants in common each own an *undivided* interest in the whole parcel of land, which means that none of the heirs can claim any specific piece of land. As tenants in common, each heir has equal rights to use and occupy the land.
- As co-owners of the property, any of the tenants in common can bring an action in court asking for partition of the property.
- The Partition of heirs' property Act in Texas. The UPHPA is codified in the Texas Property Code, Title 4, Chapter 23A. The UPHPA allows co-owners in possession of property to partition the property by sale if it cannot be partitioned in kind. A partition by sale results when property cannot be easily divided into equal parts
- There are two ways a court can partition or divide the property: partition in kind or partition by sale. If a court orders partition in kind, the land must be physically divided equitably and proportionate to the fractional interest and value of each co-owner's share. If the court orders partition by sale, it triggers a process that requires the property to be sold.
- It is very important for heirs' property owners to make sure property taxes are paid in full because tax sales can lead to loss of land. Property becomes subject to a tax sale when a landowner fails to pay annual property taxes on time. The overdue amount generally becomes a tax lien, which may cause the local government authority to begin a process to sell the land.
- Adverse possession allows a trespasser to become the owner of land they do not own if they meet certain criteria and bring an action in court asking a judge to declare them the owner. Failure to monitor and manage heirs' property can invite neighbors and others to develop a strong case for seeking ownership of land in this way. To avoid this, "No Trespassing" signs should be posted, and if a family member cannot check the land periodically, a manager should be hired.

- "Possession" means that the person has been cultivating the land, has fenced all the land, or has improved the land in some way such as building structures, planting timber, or other activities that add to its value. In Texas, the possession must also be "peaceable," meaning that the original owner has not filed suit during the statutory period to recover the property.
- Texas heirs' property owners should know that there are circumstances under which a co-tenant heir can attempt to gain sole title to heirs' property based on adverse possession against another co-tenant heir.
- For example, a person can claim adverse possession of land they co-own with other heirs after living on the property and paying taxes for at least ten years if no other co-tenant has done anything to establish their ownership of the property.
- The co-tenant heir seeking title under adverse possession must give the other co-tenants notice, including publishing notice in a local newspaper, and must file affidavits in the county offices where deed records are kept. The co-heirs have five years to file an affidavit objecting to the co-tenant's claim of adverse possession or file a lawsuit to recover their interests
- Condemnation occurs when the local, state, or federal government forces a landowner to sell their land to the government. State and federal governments, local city and county governments, and private businesses can take private land under "eminent domain" laws if they can show that doing so is necessary for a public use or purpose.

Appendixes – Easements

The following definitions are from multiple sources and are not specific to any particular state statute. Of course, any statutory definitions (terms defined in the laws of a particular state) would overrule these definitions in any legal proceeding

- An *easement* is a means by which a landowner grants another person the right to use the landowner's property for a specific purpose. The land on which the *easement* is granted is referred to as the *servient estate*, and the land the easement benefits is referred to as the *dominant estate*.
- A property owner cannot block an *easement* if it was already mentioned in the property's deed. If the property owner attempts to contest the *easement's* boundaries, then a property survey is warranted.
- An *express easement* is the most common type of *easement* that an individual or entity can obtain. The latter *easement* can be structured via a grant or reservation. When an *express easement* is granted, the landowner provides another party with the ability to use their land for right of way purposes.
- Texas law recognizes an *easement* in specific circumstances when it is necessary to cross another property owner's land. *Easement by necessity* requires proof from the party seeking the *easement.*
- Without a written document, an *easement* may be created three ways. They are (a) by *implication,* (b) by *estoppel,* and (c) by *prescription.*
- *Easements* generally fall under two broad categories: *express* (meaning *easements* expressly granted by one party to another) and *implied* (meaning easements granted by operation of law when certain facts are present)

- A *prescriptive easement* is a legal right enjoyed over another's freehold property and which is obtained through long use. A *prescriptive easement* is similar to adverse possession. However a *prescriptive easement* relates to a right to use another person's property in a particular way as opposed to claiming ownership of the land.